PURE THOUGHTS PUBLISHING PRESENTS

THINK ON THESE THINGS

TERESA RICHARDSON

INSPIRATION, STRENGTH, GROWTH

THINK ON THESE THINGS

TERESA RICHARDSON

PTP

Pure Thoughts Publishing, LLC

Copyright

Buss, D. M. (1995) *The Evolution of Desire; Strategies of Human Mating*, Basic Books. All rights reserved.

ISBN: 978-1-943409-34-1

Printed in the United States of America.

Table of Contents

THINK ON THESE THINGS

THINK ON THESE THINGS

THINK ON THESE THINGS

THINK ON THESE THINGS

This is Just the Beginning...

The seed that God planted in me years ago has finally bloomed into a beautiful work of art. What started as just a few pages of scriptures and brainstorming notes is now a book of inspiration. God blessed me with a promotion at my current job that placed me around strong women of God. It was not long before they began viewing my work and slowly pushed me to share this gift with the world. Doubt, hesitation, and fear set in and it delayed what God had already ordained. Throughout the years, I always was inspired by the way Jesus used parables to "break down" his word. In 2012, I decided to create my own little devotional book to encourage others as they encounter issues in life. I knew what I wanted to say, but hesitated almost a year because of my inner fear. The Lord spoke to me one night and brought back his word in Habakkuk 2: 2-3: "And the Lord answered me, and said, Write the vision, and make it plain upon tables, that he may run that readeth it. For the vision is yet for an appointed time, but at the end it shall speak, and not lie; though it tarry, wait for it; because it will surely come, it will not tarry." I knew at that moment that it was time to Birth my Book! I am confident that this is my appointed time. With the prayers of my family, friends and church family,

I am finally able to present to you, in my own way, what God has implanted inside of me through his word and personal experiences of my own. This is not the typical devotional, but it will encourage and empower you to stand and be what God has called you to be. We all go through rough times, and I pray that this book brings life to your situations and encourages you to hold on to his promises. We are living in the last days, and now more than ever, we need to pray and draw closer to Christ. I pray that you enjoy this book of inspirations explained in my way. It is true that "your gift will make room or you". It's time to unwrap this gift. Get ready, set, read and be empowered by the word of God!!!

*Special thanks to all of my family, my local and extended church family, my coworkers and friends for encouraging me throughout this process. It has not been easy, but I am forever grateful to God for allowing me to get this far. Pray that this will be a blessing to you. To my pastor/father, Bishop Nathaniel Dixon Sr.-words cannot express how grateful I am to sit under your ministry and hear the uncut word of God. Thank you for pushing me to pray and fast concerning this book. God has stirred up this gift and I am happy to share it with the world. God bless you, daddy!

"But these are written, that ye might believe that Jesus is the Christ, the son of God; and that believing ye

THINK ON THESE THINGS

Turn the Light On!

"Then spoke Jesus again unto them, saying, I am the light of the world; he that followeth me shall not walk in darkness, but shall have the light of life." –John 8:12

In 1989, Hurricane Hugo tore through South Carolina and left everyone dazed and confused. Those strong winds left a lot of damage and caused a great power outage across the state. I was 8 years old at the time, but I remember all of my family huddled into the den waiting for the storm to pass over. The lights went out and all we had to use was flashlights and candles that we burned throughout the night. Imagine being in a dark room and the only thing that you can depend on is the light of a candle or flashlight. It was scary, but that was the only source of light until the power company gave us relief the next day.

Jesus Christ is the source of light that we need in order to make it through the dark times. Sometimes it may seem that the storms of life are raging and you may feel like giving up, but don't! Hold on, and trust the words of Christ. He promises to never leave or forsake us. John 8:12, encourages us to follow him, and we shall not walk in darkness, but we will have the light of life. We have a responsibility to let our light shine. The light of Christ shining in us lets the world know we are children of the most high and we are redeemed.

THINK ON THESE THINGS

Matthew 5:16 "Let your light so shine before men, that they may see your good works, and glorify your father which is in heaven. This is a great way to witness to others without saying a word. Others will glorify God when they see him working through you. The light of Christ not only shines when you are in church, but also outside of the four walls of the sanctuary. Everywhere we go, we have a charge to let or light shine. Your light may shine as you witness to someone in need, encourage someone who is feeling down, volunteer at a local shelter or soup kitchen, checking on the elderly and praying for the sick that God will heal and restore them completely.

Luke 8:16 plainly declares that "no one, when he has lit a lamp, covers it with a vessel or puts it under a bed, but sets it on a lampstand, that those who enter may see the light." It is imperative that we continue to let the light of Christ shine in us. There is no need to hide what he has planted inside of us when we accepted him as Lord and Savior. There are many people walking in darkness looking for a light to lead them in the right way. As believers, we can draw others to Christ with the light that shines within us.

If you are reading this and you don't know Christ in the pardon of your sins, it's not too late! Accept Jesus Christ today, repent of your sins and let the light of Christ shine as you live a life of righteousness and obedience to him.

THINK ON THESE THINGS

Others will see the Christ in you and draw closer to him. Once you have accepted him, you will never be in the dark again. Christ is the light. Turn the light on! "Ye are the light of the world. A city that is set on a hill cannot be hid." –Matthew 5:14

Hang on in There!

"But he that shall endure to the end, the same shall be saved": -Matt 24:13

Situations may arise in our lives that cause us to feel completely defeated. Many times we would rather give up than to endure tough trials and tribulations. Giving up seems like the only option, but wait! God has got a plan and I want to encourage you to hang on in there. It seems like the more we try to do better, the more intense the trials get. Once one storm is over, here comes another one. Those rough situations leave some of us spiritually and mentally exhausted. In these times, it is very important to remain prayerful and "hang on in there" because every test we encounter is not in vain. This is easier said than done, but there is a purpose and a lesson in every trial that we go through. The Word of God encourages us to rejoice in tribulations. James 1:12 talks about the crown of life that Christ promises to all believers that endure. With that being said, it is easy to rejoice as we go through because we know in the end we will have the victory. You may not be able to see the finish line, but have faith that it is there, and hold on just a little while longer. Sometimes we have to go through certain things in order to get to the place where God wants us to be. It is a requirement, so we have to endure in order to move forward in Christ.

THINK ON THESE THINGS

I pray that when those rough situations arise, you hang on in there with all that you've got-you may feel like throwing in the towel, but wait! Help is on the way! As you go through, try not to dwell on the uncomfortable feeling you have and stop wondering how long this is going to last. Instead, redeem the time by building your faith, and increasing your prayer life so that you will gain a better understanding of why you are going through. There is greatness in you! There are many ministers and pastors that can testify that in order to be elevated in God there was a price. Yes, God may have called them to preach, but they had to go through some rough times and some dry seasons in order to get to where Christ wanted them to be. How else can they preach the word about different situations if they had not experienced some of the trials that come along with it? It may be uncomfortable, but I challenge you as a believer to hold on and possess the confidence that he is God and he is right there and will guide you every step of the way.

Ephesians 6:9 "and let us not be weary in well doing, for in due season we shall reap if we faint not.

May I Have Your Attention, Please?

Sometimes we are so caught up in our busy lives, we neglect the important things. Everything happens for a reason, but sometimes things happen to get our attention. Ever sat in a classroom and the principal comes on the loudspeaker with important announcements? The teacher makes sure everyone is quiet so they won't miss any important information. Often times God is speaking to us, and we are too tied up with the cares of this world, that we miss what he is saying to us concerning our lives. God spoke to me today and I want to share with you the things he wants you, the readers, to know. God wants to know from his people "May I have your attention please?" God is speaking, but is anyone listening?

I have heard many people say they don't believe in God because they can't see him. Many miracles that were performed in the bible days alone prove the magnificent power of the living God. Some of the greatest gifts from God are the ones that cannot be seen. The air that we breathe cannot be seen, but it allows us to live from day to day. As we travel to and from, his grace and mercy covers us from unseen dangers. God has cattle on a thousand hills, he promised to give us the desires of our hearts if we would only trust in him and live according to his word. So, why are so many believers afraid to take God at his word?

He is the same God that worked miracles and fulfilled his will through the apostles and prophets in the bible days. There is nothing new under the sun! He is the same God and if he was able to work miracles back then, he can do it now! God is challenging us to exercise our faith and take him at his word. Many people, believe the rumors and gossip about others,

end on a certain day, but won't believe the word which clearly states "no man knoweth the day nor the hour…" We believe the weather forecaster when they predict rain, snow, sleet, etc but we can't believe that GOD will do what he said.

Sometimes the weatherman is wrong but the very next day we take them on their word again. God is saying "may I have your attention, please?" He has plans for us, he wants to use us, he wants to speak to us but we have to be still and listen. He is able to be our provider, so why not trust and obey him?

The word of God plainly tells us "But my God shall supply all your needs according to his riches in glory." The word is filled with promises by God for his people and yet we are hesitant to take him at his word. God wants our attention. In times like these, we need to draw closer to him. So much is going on in this world and it seems to get worse as our days grow shorter. God is soon to come and he is demanding that we stand tall and proclaim his word. We have a responsibility to stand as one and be what God has called us to be.

My friend, I know you feel unworthy because you strayed away or did things that were not in his will, but I want to encourage you as you are reading this, God is waiting…he is standing with open arms. God is saying "I am able to fulfill your heart's desire if you would just trust in me, lean on me, draw closer to me and I will show myself mighty in your life". Do you believe it? Then act on it! He wants to heal those emotional scars, lift you up and use you to his glory. God is speaking, are you listening?

What's My Reward?

Teachers often reward their students for hard work and dedication. Sometimes they promise to give a great reward if they complete an assignment or pass a test. In the 2nd chapter of Joel, the word of God plainly describes the many things that Christ has for his people. It speaks about the latter rain, and encourages us to rejoice and be glad because surely he has great things in store for us. The prophet also declared that everyone that calls on the name of the Lord shall be saved.

Trials come, situations arise, and the load gets heavy at times in our lives. Throughout these trials, it is good to remain positive and rejoice in knowing that this too shall pass. This is easier said than done, but as we continue to read his word, we gain confidence that God will take care of us no matter how rough the situation. The Lord declares in his word that we should rejoice in him because he is going to restore the years that the locust have eaten. The things that we go through will not be in vain. Every test brings forth a testimony. There is a lesson in every storm that he allows us to go through. God has promised great things for us. For all the years we have suffered loss, suffered disappointments, handled severe storms, and suffered persecution, he promises to restore us and we will know that he is God. There will be no doubt that he will do great and mighty things in our lives. The best is yet to come!

THINK ON THESE THINGS

God is a rewarder to those that diligently seek him. The greatest reward to all believers is the crown of life which is promised to every believer who is found without spots or wrinkles as the word declares. It is imperative that we endure and remain focused because the reward is in the making. He promises in Joel 2:26 that we will eat plenty, and will be satisfied and we will never be ashamed.

Let us be encouraged and allow the love of Christ to dwell richly in each of us. If we continue to hold on and obey his commandments, our reward will be great.

Pack Your Bags!

Preparing to move to a new location requires lots of time and patience. Moving involves gathering items to pack, loading items to move, labeling everything, and of course unpacking once you arrive at your new location. Sometimes there are neighbors, close relatives and friends that don't really want us to move, and it is hard to leave them behind.

A lot of times the past haunts us, and tends to follow us as we try to move forward in Christ. People also try to bring up the past to discourage us or to cause us to feel bad about the things that we once did. God has forgiven us for the sins we committed in the past, and he has cast them into the sea of forgetfulness. Why are so many believers carrying around things of the past?

There comes a time in our lives when we must learn to put the past aside and continue on our Christian journey with no regrets, no distractions, and no thoughts of what happened in the past. The past is called the past for a reason. I want to encourage someone reading this to bury the past, and move forward to your destiny in Christ. It's time to pack! Pack all the things of the past and leave them at the altar. Leaving them at the altar brings forth freedom in our lives and we can give ourselves completely to Christ. In Phillipians3; 14,the word speaks about forgetting what is behind and striving towards what is ahead. This is great advice for all believers. God wants to flourish us with an abundance of blessings and elevate us to a new level in him, but he does not want us to bring the old baggage from the past. There is no room in our future for your past. It is time to let go, let the past stay in the past and allow God to reign in every aspect of our lives.

Allowing the past to control us hinders us from moving forward in Christ. He has so much for us, we don't want to waste time dwelling on the past or allowing others to throw our past in our face. The enemy sees our future and will do anything he can to hang our past over our head and make us believe we are not worthy to have the things that God has prepared for us. So, leave the past behind, and move forward to the wonderful things that he has in store for us.

When the Way is Not Clear

Have you ever been in heavy fog early in the morning or late at night? It seems like the more you travel into the fog the heavier it gets. The way is not clear, so we slow our speed and feel our way through the fog. Even with the bright lights on, it's hard to see your way. Often times in our lives, we encounter rough/foggy times where it seems there is no end. The more we try to do better in our Christian walk, the tougher the trials get. We tend to slow down in our walk with Christ because we are not sure what the outcome is or what is on the other side of our foggy situation. Fear begins to set in because we are unsure as to what is ahead.

Proverbs 29; 25 talks to us about fear and also reminds us that if we continue to trust in the Lord, we will be kept safe. There is no need to fear when going through rough times because God is our light and salvation. He will be the light to clear our path and will provide direction when we don't quite know where to go or how to make it through the thickness of our storms.

My friend, I want to encourage you to exercise your faith during these times and reach out to God. He will guide you all the way through and before you know it, the way will be clear and you will be able to walk out of that storm/foggy situation with V-I-C-T-O-R-Y in your hand! Your faith and prayer work hand in hand. Use your faith and continue to pray as you go through life. Sometimes you may not be sure of the outcome, but be sure of one thing-God will bring you out. He is the light of the world, so there is no need to fear! You are an overcomer!

Psalm 27:1 "The Lord is my light and my salvation; whom shall I fear? The Lord is the strength of my life; of whom should I be afraid?"

In the Midst of Anger

Have you ever witnessed a fight or heated argument? It seems as if the opponents were so angry and wanted to harm the other person in the worst way. A lot of times we engage in arguments or brawls with others but don't know the real reason why we argued to begin with. Is it even worth it? What is to be gained by arguing or engaging in a fight? Life happens, and as a believer we have to be equipped to handle situations like these in the right way.

Colossians 2:13 "Forbearing one another, and forgiving one another, if any man have a quarrel against any: even as Christ forgave you, so also do ye." This verse is the perfect remedy to any issues believers have with other believers or anyone that they encounter problems with. Remember we are representatives for Christ and we must do things as he would. Just as Christ forgave our sins, we have to forgive our brother or sister no matter what they have done to us. That's why verse 15 of Colossians 2 tells us to let the peace of God rule in our hearts. With God's peace, we can handle any situation without getting out of character or down right angry.

Have you ever lashed out at someone or said anything mean to someone? How did you feel later after you have cooled down? Did you regret saying those things or acting in anger? Of course we have feelings of regret but at the moment we only think about it doing things to make the other person feel the pain that we feel. We lose focus of Christ's instructions to love one another and we gain thoughts of revenge and evil.

As Christians, we must always remember there are others watching us. There maybe someone that wants to know Christ and the very moment we step out of character, it drives them away. Be slow to speak in these situations, and also as a turtle moves at a slow pace, we must be slow to anger as the word tells us.

No matter who is at fault, make things right and move on. Everything that we go through provides us with a valuable lesson. We learn from our mistakes, and we gain knowledge in that specific area. Christ spoke to us concerning this in James 1:19-20. "So, then, my beloved brethren, let every man be swift to hear, slow to speak, slow to wrath; for the wrath of man does not produce the righteousness of God." We realize that we were once in darkness and now we are in the light of the Lord. We must walk as children of light and walk in love, compassion, and forgiveness.

I challenge each of you to take one day and write down every person you have an issue with past or present-whether you are at fault or not. For the next week, pray for them! Release any anger and ill feelings, and allow God to cleanse your heart and mind so you will walk in love and forgiveness.

THINK ON THESE THINGS

Driving in the Wrong Lane

Have you ever gone on a road trip and got off on the wrong exit? Have you ever lost your way and you passed the exit that would have led you home? One of my close friends, Pastor Travis Laws, shared this on a recent blog and I want to share it with each of you to encourage you to let God lead you.

One of the reasons so many of us are unfulfilled is that we are driving in the wrong lane. We operate in the lanes of life that were NEVER designed for us. We operate in purposes that were never designed for us. All exits are good exits, but not all exits are OUR exits. It may be the right path for someone else but not specifically for us. We should only get off on exits because they take us to our intended destination. This is also where prayer comes in. God directs our paths and helps us get to our destinations if we would trust him and let him guide us in every aspect of our lives.

Many of us are missing our purpose because we took any old exit where we saw a light (maybe it was to satisfy a feeling of loneliness, a sexual craving, a reputation, or simple stoke of our ego). We should only take exits that take us toward our destiny, not away from it. The exits in life that God intends for us to take move us toward our destiny, our purpose or calling. Sometimes finding our way back to the main road may seem impossible, but with God all things are possible. Psalms 32:8 "I will instruct thee and teach thee in the way which thou shalt go: I will guide thee with mine eye."

Lately, people have been using the phrase "stay in your own lane" meaning mind your own business or to alert them that this is not their usual territory. I want to use the phrase "stay in your lane" to signify stay in the lane that God has designed for you and he will direct our paths. Even when the way seems dark, he is the light of the world, so we must keep our faith in him and be confident that he will lead us to the right exit in life.

THINK ON THESE THINGS

Spiritual Maintenance

One Sunday morning, as my Bishop concluded his sermon, he gave us a great scenario to remind us to keep Christ in our lives.

"There was a man who had a car in his driveway. Every day he would go outside and wash/wax it, shine the tires, wash the windows and clean the interior. Neighbors and those who passed by would admire this nice car. For some reason they never saw the man drive the car or even move it out the driveway. One day someone caught him outside as he was finishing up his daily maintenance, and asked to look under the hood. He was curious to see what kind of motor was in this beautiful car. It had to be the most powerful motor with the ability to race up and down the road. To his surprise, there was nothing under the hood." My bishop advised us to make sure we have Christ in our lives. We can look good on the outside and the world may think we've got it all together but if we don't have Christ, we are just like that shiny car with no motor on the inside. We are not going anywhere. That car in his scenario was beautiful but it was not equipped to move from that one spot in the driveway.

Ephesians 1:14   reminds us that God has given us his Holy Spirit as a promise that we will receive everything that he has for us. Possessing the spirit of God will fill that void-that empty place in your heart and it will cause a major change in your walk, your talk, your attitude, your view of life. He assures us in Psalm 62:11 that power belongs to him. If we have him on the inside, we have power. With him, we possess the power to move, live, and go out in the hedges and highways as mentioned in Luke 14:23 is important to make sure we are equipped with Christ so we can move through life and walk in our purpose. There is nothing to gain if we stay in one spot all the time. Just as we would wax a car to make it shine, gaining knowledge in Christ will cause our face to shine. Often times we struggle with habits or issues and it is time for a spiritual tune-up. God is able to replace those old parts with new ones. He can restore and renew our spirits. He is also able to move some things out of our lives. Some people are meant to be in our lives forever, others for just a season. As a part of our spiritual maintenance, God can remove those people from our lives and plug in positive influences and encouraging people to help keep us going. This journey is not easy, but as long as we allow Christ to steer the wheel, we will never go wrong. Believers, it's time to crank up, and be on the move for Christ!

"But indeed for this purpose, I have raised you up, that I may show my power in you, and that my name may be declared in all the earth." Exodus 9:16

Keeping the Body in Tact

At the beginning of the year, there are many commercials and sales ads that promote healthy eating and weight loss. Weight loss is a very popular goal that some set each year, but never seem to stick to it. More people are trying to maintain healthy lifestyles to prevent high blood pressure, diabetes and other illnesses that try to attack the body. Good exercise and a healthy eating habit is definitely a great start to keeping our bodies in the right condition.

The church is the body of Christ and we need each other to survive. In the body of Christ, we are supposed to work together to keep the body functioning correctly. Romans 12:4 clearly states: "there are many members, but one body." Each part has a specific function and all work together to keep the blood flowing evenly throughout the body.

We have to be careful what we allow in our natural bodies. Everything is not good for us. If we digest the wrong thing, it could cause the body to become severely contaminated and may develop into a disease. Diseases of the body can cause major damage. This is why we, as people of God, have to keep our spiritual body in maintenance with prayer and supplication. The Word of God that comes to us each Sunday morning acts as a supplement that keeps us spiritually filled and ready to defeat the enemy.

THINK ON THESE THINGS

A lot of ministries are allowing the enemy to creep in the back door and it is causing major issues in the body of Christ. Some pastors are compromising to gain membership, fame, or popularity. Gospel singer Micah Stampley presented a song called "You can't compromise just to fit in" and the lyrics speak about how many people are compromising just to fit in or to gain things when in reality they are contaminating the body of Christ.

If the head was anointed to preach the word and the hands were anointed to minister through song, why would one get jealous or envious of the other? The hands would end up choking the head and this will slow the blood flow and affect not just the head, but the entire body. The legs should not get mad and cut off the arms because they don't get along. If this happens, it will cause confusion, and the body will then become an amputee. There are many spiritual amputees walking around in the world and some haven't even realized how much pain they are causing the rest of the body. It's almost like a jar filled with crabs- everyone is repeatedly pulling each other down not realizing that if they work together, they can all get out of that jar. In the end, nobody gets anywhere. Fighting against each other only invites envy, jealousy, selfishness, and other ungodly things to creep in. This is how the body becomes diseased. The bible speaks against ungodly things and encourages us in Galatians to possess the fruit of the spirit Remember, we need each other to survive. I encourage everyone reading this to embrace the gift or talent that you have, and let it grow-God will provide the increase and the body will function as it should. Keep God first, and everything will fall into place.

Access Granted

In order to gain access to almost anything, there is something required. It may be a password, an ID card, an entrance fee, or even a simple key. One day, as I was scanning my badge to get into my building at work, I thought about how easy it is for us to access heaven.

Joel 2; 32 declares that anyone that calls on the name of the Lord shall be delivered. See, easy access! Throughout the bible, we are reminded of God's promises and how easy it is to gain access to heaven and the benefits of being a child of God. Often times we stray away or may fall, but it is good to know that Christ is faithful to forgive, restore, and use us to his glory. Christ commands us to love one another (even our enemies) and to obey his commandments. Salvation is free, but why are many people not taking advantage of it? If Christ died to wash our sins away, why are some people still living a sinful life?

It is our job to spread the good news of Jesus to everyone. We have to learn to let our light of Christ shine within us every day so others can see the God in us and glorify the father. Everything that we do, it should be to the glory of the father. This is a great way to draw others to Christ. If we can encourage the unbeliever to make the first step, God promises to do the rest. He will take care of them and as a gardener takes care of his garden, he will keep them nourished and daily shower them with righteousness and love.

Prayer is the key and faith unlocks the door. God is able to provide access to eternal life. The road is not easy, but at times when life brings us to tears and our back is against the wall, his word in Psalms 126:5 gives us confidence that if we sow in tears, we shall reap in joy. The joy of the lord gives us strength to carry on and as time goes on, it gets easier and easier.

Slow as a Turtle

In the story of the tortoise and the hare, the tortoise moved at a very slow pace, but in the end he won the race. Sometimes it may seem that the fastest person has the victory, but moving at a slow pace is often the best way to be especially when it comes to conversations.

Often times we get into the wrong company or simply end up in the wrong place at the wrong time. It is important as a representative of Christ not to engage in unholy conversation. Philippians 1:27 tells us plainly to let our conversation be as it becomes the gospel of Christ. This prevents us from being drawn into a bad conversation. We should not be found gossiping about others or using bad language that is not pleasing to Christ. This is not a good image for someone who proclaims Christ. We must keep his words in our hearts and continue to present the image of Christ.

"Wherefore my beloved bretheren, let every man be swift to hear, slow to speak, slow to wrath." -James 1:19

Turtles move at a very slow pace but they are very patient, and this is an example of how we should be as believers. If we find ourselves in bad company we must continue to let our light shine. We still have to hold up the banner of Christ and show the world that we are holy. Ecclesiastes 5:6 tells us "suffer not thy mouth to cause thy flesh to sin;" Though we may want to add our "two cents" in a conversation or tempted to join in an ungodly godly session-think of the turtle…be s-l-o-w to speak or react if we have been done wrong. In the book of Judges, Delilah wanted to find out Samson's weakness so he can be subdued. Often times, people want to find out your inner secrets and weaknesses so they can defeat you. This is why we must be slow to speak. All the time, Delilah was back and forth revealing things to the rulers of the Philistines and in the 18th verse, they shaved his head and were able to seize him. This is when his strength left him and his weakness was revealed to everyone. Sometimes what we reveal can get us into trouble, this is why Christ encourages us to be slow to speak. Even if something happens where we feel that we are not wrong, don't be swift to defend yourself. Take a moment and think, then respond. Proverbs 14:29 : " He that is slow to wrath is of great understanding; but he that is hasty of spirit exalteth folly." Ask the Lord to guide your words, your thoughts, and respond in a way that would be pleasing in his sight.

How Bad Do You Want It?

In this society, many are wrapped around the "see it to believe it" mentality. If they are not able to see it, it is hard to fully believe that something is real or is going to happen. In the bible days, people were more likely to believe because Jesus was there in the flesh and the miracles were performed in their view. Matthew, chapter 8 verses 1-4 tells a brief story of how the leper was healed instantly by Jesus. "And behold, there came a leper and worshipped him, saying Lord, if thou wilt, thou canst make me clean." This man saw Jesus and the multitudes coming down from the mountain and made a simple request. Often times we hesitate to ask for things and we end up missing out on our blessings. My mother always told me, just ask! The worst a person could say is no! This is so true and as you read more into the story, Jesus shows us how he answers the leper's simple request to be healed. "And Jesus put forth his hand, and touched him, saying, I will; be thou clean. And immediately his leprosy was cleansed. And Jesus saith unto him, See thou tell no man; but go thy way, shew thyself to the priest, and offer the gift that Moses commanded, for a testimony to them."

Everyone in the area knew of the leper's condition and it was probably normal to see him walking around with his skin looking chaffed and diseased. Jesus wanted this man to go about his business as usual and when the people see him, they will immediately know that he was healed. If the leper never asked Jesus to heal him, he would have still been a leper. His healing was proof to the people that Jesus is a healer. The woman with the issue of blood in Mark 5 also had one simple request. She desired to be made whole and she pushed until she got to Jesus and when she touched him, she was healed immediately. Hezekiah had one simple request in 2 Kings. He turned his face to the wall and prayed for it. God honored his request and added 15 more years to his life!

If there is something that we desire, all we have to do is ask. There is no need to hesitate or be afraid. He welcomes us to come to him and ask what we will. How bad do you want it? How long have you been dealing with that issue you can't seem to shake? How long have you been crying at night not knowing which way to turn? My friend, all it takes is one simple request. Hebrews 4:16 encourages us to come boldly to the throne of grace. Be mindful not to ask things amiss, but go to him fervently and he is able to bring forth deliverance, healing, and freedom.

I Chronicles 4:10 "And Jabez called on the God of Israel, saying, Oh that thou wouldest bless me indeed, and enlarge my coast, and that tine hand might be with me, and that thou wouldest keep me from evil, that it may not grieve me! And God granted him that which he requested."

Christ is the Solid Foundation

When contractors build homes the first thing that they survey is the land. The foundation has to be right before they can start building. If the land is not stable, then the building process cannot begin.

Psalm 11:3 "If the foundations be destroyed, what can the righteous do?" This is a good question. If a house is built and a storm comes and wipes everything away, how can one pick up the pieces? What can we do to make sure we are building on a solid foundation? As believers, we have to be sure that the foundation we are building on is secure and firm. On a firm foundation, believers can build upright and become what God has called us to be. We can stand strong and not be fearful when the enemy comes to destroy us.

The big, bad wolf would definitely be a symbol of the devil himself. 1 Peter 5:8 describes him as a roaring lion, seeking whom he may devour. He is lurking around trying to see how many believers he can distract and how many lives he can destroy. Some people have their houses built on sand and when the enemy comes, the entire structure will fall. This foundation is not sturdy and just as the first little pig who built their house with straw, it can easily be torn down and everything inside exposed. Some have a form of godliness, similar to the pig that had a house made of wood, but deny the power thereof. We should aim to have a solid foundation just as the pig who built their house with bricks. Matthew 7:24-25 speaks of a man that built his house upon a rock. When the wind and the rain came to beat on the house, it did not fall. It was founded upon a rock.

Having a firm foundation assures us as believers that no weapon formed against us shall prosper. Christ is that solid rock that we should build upon. He will not let us lean to the right or the left but go forward. Isaiah 59:19: "When the enemy shall come in like a flood, the Spirit of the Lord shall lift up a standard against him." Even if we have experienced a storm that destroyed the house we once built up, God is able to pick up the pieces and begin the restoration process. He will lift us up and place us upon a solid rock so that when the storms of life begin to rage, we will stand. From that point, we can grow into what God has called us to be.

"Nevertheless the foundation of God standeth sure, having this seal, the lord knoweth them that are his…" – 2 Timothy 2:19

A Disease called F-E-A-R

A group of young baseball players have been practicing all week for a big game. The game day has arrived and the players are in position ready to win. The visiting team comes on the field and immediately, all the young players began to doubt their abilities to win because the other team members are much taller and intimidating. The coach gives them a pep talk and reminds them that they are all capable of winning, but the players let the image of the opposing team wash away their hopes to win the big game. The team members want to forfeit the game and go home.

Fear is one of the deadliest diseases of the mind. It may start out with one thought or one negative word from someone else. If we entertain it, it spreads like wildfire and paralyze goals and dreams. Once the seed of fear enters the mind, it can cause distress, anxiety, worry, panic, and other dangerous things to enter the mind and cause issues. There are thousands of people in this world that have brilliant inventions and world changing ideas, but never let the world see them because fear has caused a standstill on their dreams.

The Word of God instructs us to fear is when it is concerning him. We are not to fear anything or anyone but God. We are instructed to fear the Lord our God. He delights in those that fear him. Psalms 19:9 "The fear of the Lord is pure, enduring forever..." Psalm 110:10 "The fear of the Lord is the beginning of wisdom." On a personal note, I had a habit of starting great projects, or ideas and never completing them. I struggled with fear for many years and I wondered if people would like my idea, or would they criticize it or laugh. As I grew older, I realized that people's opinion didn't matter when it came to my dreams and goals. Writing this inspirational book was a struggle, I questioned its value and often asked for other people's views, but with God's help I completed it!

There is no need to fear what man can say or do to us. This cripples our minds and causes us top hesitate when doing things for Christ. Some people may hesitate in witnessing to others because they fear if the person would accept what they say or not. In Hebrews 13:6, Christ lets us know we can say with confidence that he is our helper. He assures us that he has our back and will not let our enemies consume us. David wrote in the book of Psalms many times about his fears of his enemies and how they want to devour him, but God reassures us that he is God and that he can make our enemies our footstool. "The Lord is my light and my salvation, whom shall I fear?" 2 Timothy 1: 7 tells us that "God has not given us a spirit of fear, but of power and of love and of a sound mind." So why are so many people allowing the disease of fear cripple our mind and bring fear in our hearts? Why do we allow people and things to limit us and cause us to hesitate when achieving our hopes and dreams? When fear tries to creep into our minds, that's when our spirit will rise up and destroy those thoughts of fear, despair, and confusion because the joy of the Lord is our strength! As believers, we have to pray continually for strength to defeat the spirit of fear and the boldness to go on. Our strength comes from God's favor not from man's opinion about what should or shouldn't be. Be strong and bold in the Lord, and confident that the dream or thought you want to birth will make a difference in someone's life. Let's defeat fear with the power of Christ's love. It's time to stand and be what God has called us to be. Let love overtake our hearts and minds because there is no fear in love. Love conquers all, and it is the best medicine to cure the disease of fear, and any negative things that may enter into our minds and hearts. Heaven is our main goal and we must work towards it.

Psalms 34:7v   "The angel of the Lord encamps around those who fear him, and he delivers them."

THINK ON THESE THINGS

Are you a Good Samaritan?

I John 3:17 "but whoso hath this world's good, and seeth his brother have need, and shutteth up his bowels of compassion from him, how dwelleth the love of God in him?"

You are running a few minutes late for Sunday service and as you are riding, notice a man lying on the side of the road. He is bleeding, and needs immediate attention. Would you stop and pick this stranger up, or just keep going? The first thing most people would consider would be the fact that the man is a complete stranger, and that you don't know what the issue is with him. So, would you stop and help the man, or keep going and pray that someone else would pick him up?

In Luke 10, Jesus gave a great parable of the Good Samaritan. Christ used this story to influence his followers to have mercy on those in need as the Good Samaritan did. Verse 30 tells us more about this mystery man. This man had been robbed, beaten, and left for dead. A priest and a Levite both passed by and saw this man, but did not stop to see about him. This is the way some believers are. We profess Christ, but when it comes to witnessing to others in need or lifting someone up when they are down, we pass by the person   just like the Levite and the priest. We often use the phrase "I will just pray for them," but never get in there and do legwork to help others get the help they need. Jesus did not mean for us to physically stop and pick up everyone we see on the side of the road, but he told this parable to make a simple point-help others in need. Someone may not be physically lying on the road, they may be spiritually down, emotionally burdened, may have fallen astray, or may not know Christ at all.

Jesus shared the good news to everyone he met. He performed many miracles and was not stingy with the type of men/women he helped. If we have it, and see someone in need, we should be as the Good Samaritan and help them. As a believer, we never know what a person is struggling with or may be in need of. There may be some that will try and take advantage of our kindness or generosity, but there are many that are truly in need of financial, spiritual, or physical help. Think about it for a moment. Someone may be on the verge of committing suicide and one encouraging word from you may save their life. We have a major responsibility as believers/representatives for Christ. We have to remember that we were not always saved. We were not saved from birth-someone had to help us find our way and get to the point where we are today. So, why not help someone else in need? There are many that take advantage of our kindness, I challenge you to reach out to someone in need. Whether you pray with them, witness to them, help them financially, or just giving them a hug-it means a lot and God will be pleased with your sincerity. You may be entertaining angels unaware! Read Luke 10:25-37 and apply it to your life.

THINK ON THESE THINGS

The Table is Set

The table is set, are you ready to be fed? Sometimes the menu is something we don't like, or maybe it is something hard to swallow, but it is much needed to survive in times like these. My friend, I want to share with you a scenario that came to me and hopefully it will help you understand what God has set up for you.

The table represents a believer's salvation. It holds everything together. It is sturdy, it is large and able to hold even the heaviest dish. Of course it is covered by a silk tablecloth. Some tables have fruit bowls as decoration. On this table the fruits that are arranged in the bowl all make up the fruit of the spirit. We know the fruit of the spirit is love, joy, peace, longsuffering, gentleness, meekness, gentleness, and temperance.

God has set the table before us. He allowed his son Jesus Christ to die on Calvary to release us and to remove our sins. We now have a right to the tree of life. The utensils needed are fork, spoon, and knife. I refer to these as the knowledge, wisdom, and power. These utensils are all needed to eat. They help us devour what is set before us. It is imperative that we use these utensils to make it easier to consume the Word of God and to feast on his goodness. Remember, they all work hand in hand.

There is an empty plate on the table which represents an empty vessel. Once a sinner comes to Christ, they are a empty vessel yearning to be filled with the nutrients needed to maintain. When a sinner comes to Christ, they begin to drink milk and then graduate to the meat which is the Word of God. The menu that came to me was steak and potatoes. My friend, this scenario is being used to to let others understand exactly what God wants us to grasp, and that is

he is able to give us all we need and we can feast on his goodness for eternity. The steak is representing the Word of God. Sometimes the Word is hard to swallow and sometimes it gets rough around the edges, but it is good for you. Mashed Potatoes are commonly used when someone has steak on the menu. The mashed potatoes represent the father, son, and the holy ghost. These three work hand in hand and just as milk, butter, and white potatoes make one creamy delicious side. Don't forget the gravy-your anointing. The anointing makes a difference in every believer's life. It is imperative that the gravy is poured evenly on the potatoes. Some people have other fixings with their meal and we will just refer to them as all the ingredients a believer needs to make it.

A meal is not complete without something to wash it down right? Well, the cup that is before us is filled with water. When a believer drinks of this living water, they will never thirst again. This cup will never get empty it will continue to be filled. Thetable is set before you, are you ready to receive?

Making it Through the Storm

Sometimes the storms of this life try to consume us. It seems like everything is happening all at once and it feels like a cloud is over you. We can't see our way and you wonder when is this going to end? We have heard so many times that "trials come to make us strong". Yes, this is true, but what do we do while you are in the midst of the storm? Keep the faith, and pray that God sustain us as we go through. Remember, sometimes we have to go through things in order to get to where God wants us to be. 1 Peter 4:12 tells us not to think it strange that we go through rough times, but to rejoice because we are partakers of Christ's suffering.

We gain strength and wisdom with every test we go through. No one is exempt from going through rough times. Everyone goes through the storms of life, but it is up to us if it will consume us or if we will stand tall and makes it through the storm. It may not always feel good while we are going through, but in the end it will be well worth it. Things will be clear and we will see exactly what God has for us. So rejoice in your storm, remain in prayer, and keep the faith. Sometimes it gets too rough and giving up seems like the easy way out. But what have we learned? Did Jesus get down from the cross? He may have wanted the cup to pass, but he endured and he paid the ultimate price that gave us access to eternal life.

THINK ON THESE THINGS

My friend, the very storm that you are going through is for a specific purpose. You may feel like giving up right now, but hang on in there because there is a testimony that comes from every test. Your endurance through this storm may elevate you to a new level in God, and in the end draw millions to him through your teaching, preaching, ministry through song, or whatever he has designed you to do. God has carried you through all the other storms you encountered, so what makes this one different? I know there have been times when you felt that you could not make it, and the way seems so cloudy, but didn't God carry you through? He is the same God that did it before, so be confident that he can do it again. Go through the storm so you can get to where he wants you to be! You can make it! I believe in you! God is with you!

THINK ON THESE THINGS

Don't let the Enemy Steal your Treasure!

I want to take this time to encourage anyone reading this. Don't let the enemy steal the treasure that God has placed in you! We all know that the enemy is out to kill, steal, and destroy. His job is to kill our dreams, to tear us down, to steal what God has given us, and to destroy our future. God has instilled so many precious things inside us and it is imperative that we guard it with our lives.

My friend, your treasure can be your anointing, your spiritual gifts and talents, your joy, peace, confidence, salvation, it can be anything that God has planted inside of you. This treasure is priceless, and to have someone take that away would be devastating. Just as angry pirates search for hidden treasure, the enemy and his army is lurking around seeking who they may devour. The enemy is on his job, so it's time to be about our father's business and guard our treasure!

2 Corinthians 4:7 "But we have this treasure in earthen v essels, that the Excellency of the power may be of God, and not of us"

Trying to Blend in with the World

God wants all of us to be rooted and grounded in him so when times get rough, we will not be deceived by the world. He wants us to be sanctified, free from sin, holy and set aside. I believe this is the way it should be. If we have Christ in our lives, we should have that assurance in our hearts that "for God I live and for God I die". We know that God is our shield, our present help in the time of trouble, so we should be happy to proclaim his word boldly and share with others his goodness. We should stand out and let our lights shine so others can see his good works and glorify him. Why is it that some people try to blend in with the world after they have been saved, and sanctified? Why are some afraid to talk about the Lord when they are around certain people? Why do some people try to blend in with the ungodly crowd when they say they are a child of God? Why do they confess Christ, but still try to join in the things of the world?

The word of God declares we are in the world, but not of the world. We are set aside, sanctified and we naturally STAND OUT. "Be not conformed to this world, but be transformed by the renewing of your mind. "Transformation" means complete change: usually into something with an improved appearance or usefulness. Your image has to change, your way of thinking, everything changes when you are transformed. When you are saved, you naturally stand out.

THINK ON THESE THINGS

Imagine an army of troops standing in front of you. They are all dressed in their army green attire with black boots to match. In the midst of the troops, you notice one individual who is dressed in street clothes with a hat on backwards. Do you think that they belong in this formation? Why is the person dressed in casual clothes and not in the traditional army attire? This is the way the people of God need to stand out. People should be able to see the GOD in us and know that we are different, we are children of God. We should not try and blend in with the world or compromise our salvation to please others. Why gain the world and lose your soul? Why compromise or try to blend in with the world?

Blending is not a good habit and it is not the way God wants us to be. The word "blending" reminds me of a chameleon. This animal has the ability to change colors. Sometimes in the church, we have people that frequently change their appearance and personality to fit their surroundings. Some talk differently in front of others to fit in. Why wear a camouflage? Why try to be something you are not? When you are in Christ, you are a new creature.

No matter how hard you try, you will never blend in with the world because you are set aside. The word says you are in the world, but not of the world. So why are so many people trying to blend in with the world? We are not required to follow the standard of the world, so why are so many people doing it? There are pastors and other leaders that are blending with the world to gain membership. There are gospel singers choirs, and praise teams who try to blend by including secular sound/lyrics to get an applause or a pat on the back. When churches start to conform to the world's standards, it is like opening the back door and letting the enemy come in. Allowing the enemy to creep in only brings contamination to the body of Christ and it confuses those who are trying to come to Christ. If we continually compromise, how can the world tell the difference between sinners and saints?

What benefit can they say they have by being saved if the saved people are grooving to the world's music or sugarcoating the message to fit the worldly crowd in the back of the sanctuary? God's word never changes. As the body of Christ, we should stand out, stand tall and proclaim the message of Christ even if it makes some feel uncomfortable.

God delivered the three Hebrew boys from the fiery furnace in the bible days. Those three men stood out and refused to bow to any other God. Their faith was tested, but in the end they came out victorious! My friend, will you blend in with the world or will you STAND OUT?

The Pink Tornado

Over the years, I have heard various news reporters talk about tornadoes and how they rip through cities, destroy homes, and leave people hopeless without money or food. Tragic events such as these can leave us in a state of shock. Through it all, God is still able to restore and replenish in times like these.

I am also reminded of another tornado that can ruin lives, marriages, friendships, churches, and it can have a strong effect on how we live our lives every day. The bible says life and death is in the power of the tongue. Yes, the tongue! I call it the PINK TORNADO.

James 3 speaks about the tongue calling it a fire, an untamable thing. It is amazing how we are able to tame all kinds of animal, but cannot tame the tongue. "For the tongue can no man tame; it is an unruly evil, full of deadly poison." It can ruin marriages, ruin relationships, destroy jobs, bless and curse God out of the same mouth! This pink tornado can send us straight to Hell if we let it!

Sometimes tornadoes come unexpectedly, do major damage, and then are gone in the twinkling of an eye. Swift mouths and evil tongues can turn your world upside down! They can plant the seed of evil so fast and tear up everything around you. It can start a blazing fire and destroy all you have. When the smoke clears, you have nothing and it was all because of a small thing called the tongue.

One main ingredient in the fruit of the spirit is TEMPERANCE. That is self -control. As people of God, we can try to tame our tongue as much as we can to keep our mouth from speaking untrue things and ungodly things. We must repent daily and keep ourselves around positive people so that we will not indulge in gossip, mocking, lustful thinking, corrupt ideas, and lies. That same fire the tongue started can send you to the eternal fire and brimstone. Be watchful and careful of what you say, what conversations you indulge in, and how you repeat what others say.

Proverbs 16:24 "Pleasing words are like honey. They are sweet to the soul and healing to the ones". Let your words be a blessing to others to help them along the way.

Don't push that issue under the rug!

In life, we often have unresolved issues. Sometimes we leave issues open and sweep it under the rug. Some people are too ashamed to deal with it, some are too proud to let others know they have problems. Maybe some are too afraid to address the issue at that moment, and think it would be better to push it to the side for a while. Often times, we desire closure on a situation or relationship, but never find the time to address it. Some people don't have this problem, but there are many that do. This is not a good habit. Putting things under the rug will only cause problems later on in life. In the bible, it speaks about getting it right with our brother or sister if you have an issue or ought against them. It's better to "nip it in the bud" now than to deal with it ten years down the road.

When we push things under the rug, it will eventually create a lump. It does not go away just because you choose not to address it. Just like a child that sweeps dirt under a rug at home, that lump gets bigger and bigger over time. One day when we least expect it, we will trip over that same lump and all of your issues will come rushing out. This will not be a pretty picture. Anything is liable to come out and we will have no choice but to FACE IT. And to think, all of this could have been resolved if we had not pushed it under the rug.

THINK ON THESE THINGS

It doesn't matter what our "dirt/issue" is, let God help you resolve it. Just lean on him and ask him to handle it.

S-I-N-K-I-N-G

Sometimes it feels like everything bad happens to us all at once. Our issues seem to consume us almost like we are sinking or drowning. To me, the water can represent our issues, our problems. We may be sinking in sin, debt, stressed with life itself, broken relationships or marriages, depression, etc. Some of us feel we are in the midst of a large body of water with no land in sight and no one to call on for help. We may feel like there is no hope. But there is hope! God is right there waiting on you to call on him. I know things are sinking all around you but don't fret! I know you can't swim, but keep your head above the water a little while longer because help is on the way! It may look bad everywhere you turn; you may see no land in sight, but LOOK UP because God is with you. All you have to do is grab a hold and he will pull you out of the mess that you are in. If you call on him, he won't let you drift away. No matter how bad your issue is, no matter how deep you are in, he can rescue you.

It's time to come out of the water and grab hold to JESUS. He is able to pick you up, turn you around, place your feet on solid ground. Once you are out, it's imperative that you change. Who wants to stay in cold, wet clothes after they get out of the water? So, once God pulls us out, it's time to put on the whole armor of God and become "new" again. A songwriter once said "I was sinking deep in sin, far from the peaceful shore. Very deeply stained within, sinking to rise no more. But the master of the sea heard my despairing cry. Out of the water he lifted me, and now safe am I."

Yes, let his love lift you up. When you have tried everything and nothing can help, let his love lift you out of your troubles and put you on a solid foundation to stand. No more shackles, no more dead weight keeping you down, no longer will you be consumed with the weight of this world, and no longer will you fall into the place where you are sinking. Grab a hold to Jesus and let him lead you into that higher place.

We know we don't deserve it and we could have drowned, but his grace and mercy kept us. I am grateful for my rescue team. Don't fret my friend! Just call on the name of the Lord and he will keep you from sinking.

Are you Covered?

All of us know about life insurance policies. They have millions of benefits and there is a fee monthly to keep this insurance. I thought about God and the benefits of being covered by him. To me, it is like the greatest policy with "out of this world" benefits. The amount of coverage that you have access to is PRICELESS.

There are two types of salesman. The ones that sell us life insurance representatives are the men and women of God that give you the true word. The life representatives are the anointed people that God has chosen to spread his word. They are there to witness and share God's goodness to the world. They don't always have to be ministers and preachers. They can be simple believers that live according to God's word and they share Christ with you.

The death policies are represented by false prophets and preachers that try to lead others astray. This is not a policy that you would want to look into.

Let me tell you more about the life policy. First, this policy is laced with many benefits that you can enjoy while here on earth and even after death. Let me break it down for you. Some of the benefits are reaping of spiritual and physical blessings, favor of God , good health, wealth, joy, peace, and so much more! God promises to give us the desires of our heart and he is faithful to keep his word. We just have to exercise our faith and believe that he is able to do it. Do you believe?

The premium is your PRAISE. This premium is due daily as we live according to his word. The reason I say this is because there it POWER in your praise. There is deliverance, healing, freedom, in your praise! Barriers are broken, walls come down, there are so many things can happen when you praise God. It is crucial to make sure your premium is paid. It keeps your policy active. The more you praise God, the more blessings you reap. Make sure you keep your policy up to date, or it can lapse. Allowing the enemy creep in and distract you, discourage you, or to make you turn away from God causes a lapse in your policy. The word lapse means a break in the continuity of something. A lapse in your policy is similar to a person in Christ who backslides or turns away from God. Anything can happen while your policy is in a state of lapse. This is a very critical time. If you die during this period, there is nothing to cover you. You no longer benefit from this policy. IT IS VOID.

Don't let your insurance lapse. Continue to read your word to gain more knowledge about this policy/Christian Life and praise God in the midst of your storms, no matter what comes or what goes, no matter how hard it seems, continue to pray and give praise to God. It may not seem like you are getting anywhere but in the end you will reap more than you are reaping here on earth. It may seem that your back is against the wall and nothing is going for you, but remember Hezekiah in the bible. He turned his face to the wall and he began to cry out to God and God answered his prayers. He added 15 more years to Hezekiah's life. He can do it for you too. You are covered under his policy so why not exercise the benefits. It's yours for the asking.

When you leave this world, the policy is still active. This is where the additional benefits will actually kick in. Not only are you able to enjoy the benefits of being a Christian here on earth, you also have a lot of benefits that kick in after you die. This is the only policy I know of that has benefits you can access on earth, and after you leave earth. You have access to heaven, where there are streets paved with gold, a large mansion waiting just for you. There will be no more sorrow, pain, sickness, worry, no more trials and tribulations just peace, joy and the love of Jesus flowing through the streets of Heaven. Are you covered?

In heaven, you have access to the entire KINGDOM and you can spend eternity with God. Who can top that? No one! ALLSTATE, GEICO, GLOBE LIFE, not even the best policy here on earth can compare to the policy that God offers to you. To know Jesus and to live according to his promises is all that God requires of us. We have to present ourselves faultless before him to gain access to the treasures of heaven. Are you covered?

The Game

This scenario is designed to explain life in a different view. I know a lot of sports fans, so I decided to take my limited knowledge of football and apply it to my view concerning life and the Christian journey we are on. Sometimes we have to step "outside the box" in our thinking so we can understand the message of Christ. In the bible days, Jesus used many earthly parables to help the people understand heavenly things. I pray that this blesses someone and opens their understanding about Christ.

Take a moment and imagine standing on a football field. There are two teams suited up and ready to play. Each team has a distinct jersey to identify which side they represent. Think about it in this sense. The jerseys we wear symbolize what we represent/what we believe in. It either says UNDEFEATED CHILDREN OF GOD or DECIEVING DECIPLES OF SATAN. Whose side are you on? The football represents your salvation. Hold on to what you have, don't let nobody take it from us. Your focus should be on heaven. The cheerleaders in this game represent our church family, prayer partners, prayer warriors, and family-those who are positive influences in our lives. These people will cheer us on and encourage us as we run toward the goal which is heaven. I thank God for my cheerleaders. What about you?

THINK ON THESE THINGS

The bleachers packed with people symbolize the world. The world is watching us. In life, you never know who is watching our every move; sometimes it is hard to tell who is on our side or who is on the opposing side. Be watchful and prayerful at all times! Living right may draw others to Christ. The four quarters in the game symbolize the different stages in our lives. Right now I feel that we are living in the fourth quarter. The game is almost over. Time is winding up and God is coming sooner than we think. It's crunch time! It's time for us to stand and be what God has called us to be. It's time for us to go hard and do all we can for God before it's too late. It's time to declare his word and speak things into existence, witness to the world (those in the bleachers)- tell them to come on and join the team of Christ. We are headed to heaven and our reward is waiting on us. It may seem that the opposing team is winning and their team may seem bigger or stronger, but remember we are victorious and when we get on one accord we are unstoppable! Satan has a lot of new tricks/play that may try to take us down but we have to rebuke him and move forward in Jesus Name!

The bible declares that there are many members, but one body. There are many positions on this team, many team players in the Body of Christ. We are all KINGDOM MINDED and we are all one in Christ. He is the head and we are the body. Don't be surprised if some of our fellow team members that we thought were of God suddenly turn away and go to the opposing team. There will be a great falling away as the bible tells us and some people that wear the Christ Jersey are not really his. They are distracted by some of the people on the sidelines. There are some people that smile in your face, but stab you in the back. There are enemies lined up waiting to trip us up, but they are not in the game, they are just sideline groupies. We can't let the sideline people distract us. They mean us no good. They are strays from the enemy's team that are set to discourage us, talk about us, scandalize your name and make you think that God is not with you. Don't let them deceive you. If you do, the opposing team can come and steal the ball. I want to encourage you, my friend. No matter what, hold on to your salvation and keep your focus on Christ. There is no time out in this game, we are in it to win, and we are determined to win at any cost. I don't want to forget about the water boy. Now, the water he offers is not your ordinary water. The bible declares "if you drink of this water, you will never thirst again". There is no need to have a time out. Once you drink of that water, it replenishes you and you have strength to go on.

The bible is our play book it has everything we need to make it in. When the enemy team comes wide open at us, the play book has a remedy for that. The opposing team is very swift, they are deceiving and cunning, but we have to use what we have on the inside to avoid being consumed. They are strong and they aim to tackle us from every side, but we have to hold on and the more we read the word and gain knowledge from the "playbook" we will know the enemy's strategy and this will allow us to dodge the enemy and run toward the goal. Don't run from the enemy. There is nothing to fear! The bible declares "resist the devil and HE will flee". That's right HE will flee, not you! It's time for you to stand and be what God has called you to be: a strong unbeatable team member. Stomp on the devil and remind him to "Stay in his lane and leave you alone!"

Sometimes you may lose sight on this journey and the enemy comes in and takes what you have worked so hard to obtain. Sometimes you may stray away because the other team's play looks so good and you may even backslide.

Sometimes major things happen in our lives and it cause us to take our eye off the prize for just one second. One second can cost you your life. Remember that time waits on no one. We have no time to lose, it's all or nothing.

Remember to never let your guard down. It may seem that you are in this game alone and the enemy team is surrounding you on every side. It may seem dim like there is no way out, but all you have to do is keep a grip on your ball and LOOK UP. God is right there!! "I will lift up mine eyes to the hills from which cometh my help"... God declares in Psalm 91 "Thou shalt not be afraid for the terror by night...." Don't worry, God has your back! He has the perfect remedy for the opposing team: "a thousand shall fall at thy side, and then thousand at thy right hand: but it shall not come nigh thee"... HALFTIME IS OVER; IT'S TIME TO GET BACK IN THE GAME!! HEAVEN OR HELL...IT'S UP TO YOU!

THINK ON THESE THINGS

Using Your Weapon of Praise

The military is heavily equipped with weapons to prepare for any type of war. There is intense training to prepare and when the enemy comes in sight, weapons are pulled out and soldiers aim and fire at their target. They even have target practice to make sure all soldiers know how to handle their weapons and aim correctly at the enemy.

God has equipped us with weapons specifically designed to defeat the enemy. The Lord allows us to go through different trials and tribulations in our lives as an intense training to prepare us for battle with the enemy. As we go through these things, we gain strength and wisdom. As we come out of our storms, God desires for us to be full of joy and praise him for giving us the strength to make it through. One of the many weapons that he has given us is our PRAISE. 2 Corinthians 10:4: "For the weapons of our warfare are not carnal, but mighty through God to the pulling down of strong holds.

If there is something that you are battling with, I dare you to use your weapon of praise and God will tear down that wall. In the book of Joshua 6: 2-16, Joshua commanded the people to walk around the walls of Jericho seven times, and when the trumpet sounded on the seventh day, all the people began to shout with a great shout and the walls came down. They offered up their best praise and God gave them the city. Your praise can break chains of addition, spirits of fear, depression, loneliness, confusion, it can break chains of sickness and disease, strongholds, anything that the enemy tries to throw at us, we should be equipped and able to aim, and fire at that situation with the weapon of praise. If we give him our best praise, he will show himself mighty in our lives. I encourage you to praise him for the many things that he has done. When we all assemble together in the house of the Lord, we should all come in ready to praise! We need to join on one accord, fire our ammunition with praise and allow the Holy Spirit to dwell in the midst. The word of God confirms that when we praise, he inhabits our praises.

"I will make thy name to be remembered in all generations: therefore shall the people praise thee forever and ever." Psalm 45:17

Sticks and Stones

"O generation of vipers, how can ye, being evil, speak good things? For out of the abundance of the heart the mouth speaketh."–Matthew 12:34

Have you ever heard the phrase "Sticks and stones may break my bones, but words will never hurt me?" This was commonly said throughout my childhood and as I got older, I realized this statement was far from true. Sticks and stones may harm us physically, but words can do emotional damage and can often scar us throughout our lifetime. Emotional scars are unseen, but seem to hurt worse than visible scars and blemishes seen. Words cut like a knife-they can slice up hopes and dreams, damage confidence and self-esteem. Years of verbal abuse as a child can damage someone's adulthood and shatter things in their future. Because of this, it may be hard to love, trust, or even confide in others.

Proverbs 18 reminds us that the tongue can bring death or life. Words like "God has a plan for your life" can bring joy to one's life and words like "you will never amount to anything" will destroy dreams and tear you down even if that negative word was told to us ten or twenty years ago. There are so many actors, artists, and inventors that never brought life to their dreams because someone's words deeply cut them and left a scar that causes heartbreak and pain in the end.

THINK ON THESE THINGS

Psalms 51:15: "Open my lips, Lord, and my mouth will declare your praise." This should be the mindset that we carry each day. We should use our words to uplift, encourage and to use as an instrument of praise unto our God. God has given us the strength to handle various situations. We must activate our faith, and use those same sticks and stones and build a firm foundation able to withstand anything. We can use it as a shield and make those negative words and thoughts bounce back to their source.

Surround yourself with positive people and continue to live a spirit filled life. Even if your past was filled with word curses and emotional scars, pray to God that he will heal those scars and give you the strength to achieve those goals, make those dreams a reality, and live in your purpose with no worries, no hesitation, no doubts and the confidence to know that Christ will be with you every step of the way. Christ promises to keep us in perfect peace if we keep our minds on him.

Sacrifice Equals Positive Results

As 2016 came to a close, I began to think about what I wanted to do differently in 2072. I desired to become closer to God and allow him to use me to full capacity. God spoke to me and said "what are you willing to sacrifice to get closer to me?" At that moment, I thought about how many times I would log on to the social network and how many times I post and check statuses dozens of times a dayI clearly saw where this consumed a lot of my time and in order to get closer to him I had to work on my prayer life and read his word daily to comprehend it and clearly understand it on a deeper level. So I did not make a resolution to lose weight or travel or anything like that. I was determined to sacrifice for 90 days as a start and come boldly before God's throne seeking to be more intimate with him.

I can testify today that I am closer to Christ than I have ever been and I am glad that I made the choice to sacrifice something in order to get what I needed from the Lord. What are you willing to sacrifice? A man came up to ask Jesus in Matthew 19:16 what must he do to get eternal life. Jesus began to remind him of the commandments and when he asked what else was lacking, Jesus simply said "Sell all your possessions and give to the poor, and you will have treasure in heaven. Then come follow me."

Would this man be willing to sacrifice material things to gain eternal life and treasures in heaven? Let's be real for just a moment. If you were in desperate need of healing from a sickness and God guaranteed healing if you would sell your home and car and give it to the poor –would you do it? Would you be willing to give it all up to receive your healing? Sometimes we ask God to give us more, but we are not willing to give up anything. In order for God to use us, we have to sell out completely. Genesis 22 talks about Abraham and the sacrifice he was willing to make unto the Lord. God provided a ram in the thicket and he used it as a burnt offering instead of his son. God is able to provide everything we desire, we just have to be open and willing to do whatever it takes to receive. Often times we hesitate to give in offerings because we are worried about what bills we have to pay or how much we have to set aside for the rest of the week. When we make the ultimate sacrifice and give unto the lord, we will reap the harvest and it may be three times what we initially gave. In Genesis 26:12 Isaac planted crops in the land and the same year he reaped a hundredfold. His word shows us in so many ways that he is able to provide.

Sometimes we get so wrapped up in our jobs, families, friends, social media, and material things we forget to make time for God. If you desire to be closer to him or to learn more about becoming a better servant, you have to be willing to sacrifice something. Put aside your plate one day and just pray and meditate. Log off the internet or turn the TV off for one hour and dig deep into the word of God. Challenge yourself to sacrifice something and you will see positive results. Psalm 37:4 "Take delight in the Lord, and he will give you the desires of your heart."

THINK ON THESE THINGS

Choose Your Battles Wisely

As a newlywed, there are a lot of things that I did to hurt my marriage like argue about certain things that I did not like about my spouse. I complained and did not know that it was damaging things from the inside I didn't realize it at the time, but it made things worse when I argued and used the "silent treatment" on him when I did not get my way. In any relationship, it takes a while to adapt to another person's ways when you have been independent for so long. The more we disagreed, the more I realized how unhealthy this was especially when we had small children in the home. I did not want my kids growing up hearing their parents yelling at each other all the time. There has to be some way to get through this without arguing. I prayed about it and talked with a good friend concerning this issue. I learned quickly that I did not have to participate in every argument that I was invited to.

Have you ever been invited to a special event and could not make it? Well, it's the same thing! Every argument or ungodly conversation that we are invited to, we don't have to attend. It's all a part of choosing your battles. 1 Corinthians 7:3 tells the husband to render benevolence to his wife, and likewise the wife unto the husband. This is clearly written and since God honors marriage, he expects us to be respectful to one another. Choosing your battles defeats the enemy and allows one to live their lives free from evil and invites a welcoming spirit into the marriage. Love conquers a multitude of sin and if loving one another is considered the golden rule, it surely is one that marriages need to live by each day. It is important to choose not to engage in things that are not of God. If there is something that you feel is not right, the bible encourages us to talk to that person and clear the air. This leaves your heart free of anger, resentment, and any confusion.

Choosing your battles does not only apply to marriages, but any relationships and in every aspect of your life. The enemy knows our weaknesses and he uses certain people to initiate arguments, disagreements, and other ungodly tactics to make us step out of character and lose focus. Have you ever heard someone say "I'm going to lay my religion down"? I have heard it numerous times from believers that seem to be fed up with certain people or things, but there is no such thing! Don't do it! Don't let anyone push you to say or do things that are not of God! Yes, everyone has a breaking point, but as a believer you hold the key to the outcome of every situation. Take a deep breath, and choose not to engage in it. People will even confront you with foolishness and confusion, but as in Colossians 3:15 we have to let the peace of God rule in our hearts, and remind ourselves that we wrestle not against flesh and blood. This is not a physical thing. Ephesians 6:12 tells us that we wrestle against principalities and powers, rulers of darkness of this world, against spiritual wickedness in high places. Be encouraged. Choose your battles.

Be Not Deceived

A friend of mine shared with me an encounter she had with a minister she had met some time ago. She confided in this person regarding some rough times that she fell on. As a new believer, she looked to him for encouragement and prayer. He offered to help, but also approached her in an ungodly way. He wanted something in exchange for help. This devastated her and as a new believer, and she was shocked that a person who preached the word of God would come at her in such a way. In the bible, there were many apostles and preachers that took their job seriously and were real about what they preached and used their gifts to raise the dead, heal, bring forth deliverance, and to set free those that were bound by demonic spirits. It did not sound normal having one of these distinguished men of God talk to someone in an ungodly way, or offer something in exchange for healing, right? In these times, there are many that seem to be men and women of God, but have a motive.

We are richly blessed with warnings and instructions on how to avoid being deceived. God spoke in various scriptures concerning the end times and the things that would occur. Luke 21:8 warns us to take heed that we be not deceived: there will be many shall come in his name and as time draws near, but not to go after them. 2 Timothy 3 shares some of the things that will come in the last days, but God specifically warns us in I John 4:1 not to believe every spirit because there are many false prophets gone out into the world. Matthew 24:11 even says that they shall deceive many. To avoid being deceived, we have to watch as well as pray that we are not a victim. Many times the enemy seeks those that are weak in certain areas, and he sends his workers to prey on those that are desperate and lures them with the things that they desire.

Colossians 2:8: "Beware lest any man spoil you through philosophy and vain deceit, after the tradition of men, after the rudiments of the world, and not after Christ." The enemy is cunning and crafty, but God has forewarned us, and he is still able to give us clarity in times like these if we would only pray to him. If we, as believers, would seek the Lord before making any decisions, a lot of bad things would be avoided. I am so glad that my friend was able to see through this person and avoid being fooled. If my friend was not aware of the trick, she would have fell further away from Christ and it would cause her a world of heartache and pain.

Sometimes we look at a person's title and we trust them. They are "supposed to be a man and woman of God," but in these last days, people will give themselves titles to gain your trust and brainwash you into a web of sin and shame. This is not of God. The word tells us to try every Spirit by the Spirit. In other words, seek the Lord and ask him for direction before making any move or decision. He will direct your path. If it is not of God, he will show you and you will be able to avoid any of the enemy's tricks. God is so merciful and kind that he gives us warnings and he is always there to rescue us in the time of trouble. This is why it's imperative that we watch and pray.

Taking Care of His Own

My kids and I enjoy watching nature shows where the animals interact with other animals in their environment. My kids find joy watching these educational shows. One particular day we were watching birds and the babies adapting after coming out of the egg. I thought about how protective they are of their babies and looking at how they provide for them, I began to think about how God takes care of us. As I watched how they used their wings to cover them and provide warmth and protection, I couldn't help but think about Psalm 91.

In Psalms 91:4 God reminds us that under his wings we will find refuge; his faithfulness will be our shield. God promises to take care of his children and his word encourages us to keep the faith in all situations if we only abide in him and obey his word. In reading his word, we have a sense of comfort knowing that we are covered by God in any situation. There are many things that tangle our feet and many situations that cause us to question God-there is comfort in knowing that he is there for us. In verse 7 he firmly declares: "A thousand may fall at your side, and ten thousand at your right hand, but it shall not come near you." It doesn't matter how many times we encounter the raging storms of life, no matter how harsh the trials may seem, no matter how much pain and despair we may feel as we go through, there is comfort in knowing that he will be with us in the time of trouble as declared in Psalm 27:5.

He promises to fight for us. His word will never return void. Deuteronomy 20:4: " For the Lord your God is he that goeth with you, to fight for you against your enemies, to save you." Even when it seems like God is not there and the enemy has our back against the wall, his word declares: "We are troubled on every side, yet not distressed; we are perplexed, but not in despair; persecuted, but not forsaken cast down, but not destroyed" -2 Corinthians 4:8-12. God's word always assures us that even in the midst of our darkest situation, God he also promises to deliver us out of any situation no matter how many afflictions we may encounter. (Psalm 34:19)

For those that do not know the Lord, there is no better time than NOW to accept him as Lord and Savior. Acts 2:38 gives us 2 simple steps on how to do this; Repent, and be baptized in the name of Jesus Christ for the remission of sins. Matthew 6:33 also reminds us that once we make these steps everything else will fall into place: "seek ye first the kingdom of God and his righteousness; and all these things will be added unto you". Even if you accepted him in the past and have somehow slipped away from his presence there is still hope. Don't be dismayed or feel like you can't come back to him. In Jeremiah 3:14

he speaks directly to you "Turn, O backsliding children, for I am married unto you. I encourage you to trust God, cling to him, for he will take care of his own.

"He shall call upon me, and I will answer him; I will be with him in trouble; I will deliver him, and honor him." – Psalm 91:15

So, what's Love Got to Do With It?

Psalm 103:11 "For as high as the heavens are above the earth, so great is his love for those who fear him"
Police officers, firefighters, and emergency medical service staff across the world risk their lives every day to help those in need. They are highly trained to handle intense situations and hold the responsibility to rescue all in need. It doesn't matter if they love the person or hated them with a passion. The most important thing at the time is that someone was in need, and they must give 100% to make sure everyone is safe. So, what's love got to do with it? Well, it has everything to do with it. Jesus wants all of us to love one another and help those in need no matter who they are. He tells us in his word to love one another. He did not specify if they were considered a friend or enemy. Possessing genuine love to others is the key to a believer's walk with Christ. Walking in love allows you to have compassion for others, allows you to have a giving heart and also be humble as Christ would have us to be. Remember, there is no fear in love, and with no fear, and with God's help, anything is possible; even loving enemies.

In Matthew 5:44, Jesus urges us to love our enemies, bless those that curse us, and do good to them that hate us. How can this be? This sounds like a hard pill to swallow, but with the love of Christ residing on the inside of us, it is easy to display genuine agape love. Just as

God loves us, we should show the same love to everyone. Possessing agape love is what we should display each day no matter who we come in contact with throughout each day. This kind of love is unselfish. How is it possible to love people that despise and hate us for no reason at all? Look at the life of Christ. Jesus walked the earth and showed love to all people, even those that hated him, betrayed him, and denied knowing him. The ultimate example of love that God displays in his word lies in John 3:16. Sending his son to this world to die for the sins of all mankind –is far beyond the "call of duty", but he loved us so much that he allowed Jesus to pay the price for our sins. God's love in our heart gives us a heart for others.

Even in his darkest hour as he was being crucified, he still displayed love and asked God to forgive those that hated him and were brutally harming him. His love endures forever, so our love for Christ and all mankind should also endure forever. In a world of loneliness and despair, there is a great need for men and women who know the heart of God to spread his agape love and to encourage others to share his message of forgiveness and righteousness. There is no limit to his love. As we draw closer to the end, and as the love of many begins to wax cold, it is imperative that we keep the love of Christ burning our hearts and continue to love our neighbors as ourselves. Love is not known until it is shown.

The Bigger They are, the Harder They Fall

Ever heard the phrase "the bigger they are, the harder they fall"? This is a very true statement in most cases. In the story of David and Goliath, God proved that even though the enemy is bigger, he can still be defeated with the help of God. In 1Samuel 17, Goliath was described as a champion, and the word of God described him as a 9 foot tall giant with heavy, bronze attire. He dated someone to challenge him. Using five smooth stones, and a dose of faith and trust in the Lord, David came in and defeated Goliath proving that size is not a factor. The word of God also describes our adversary, the devil, "as a roaring lion, walking about seek whom he may devour" (1 Peter 5:8) The enemy will use anyone and anything to destroy us no matter what it takes. The word did not say he was a lion, he was described as a roaring lion. His job is to make us think that he is big and bad so we will fear him and forget the power that we possess as children of God.

Wehave to remember 2 Timothy 1:7 "God has not given us the spirit of fear, but of power, and of love, and of a sound mind. He has heavily equipped us to defeat any and all enemies. Yes, we will go through trials on this journey, but when the enemy tries to steal what God has blessed us with, we have to know how to fight back! Ephesians 6:11 plainly states in order to stand against the wiles of the devil, we have to put on the whole armor of God. Have you ever seen an army of soldiers unprepared? Well, we are the army of the Lord , so just as Goliath stood with his sword and heavy armor, we can stand with the armor God has provided to us in Ephesians 6:14-18. When bad situations arise, we have a charge to stand! Stand and girt our loins with the truth and put on the helmet of salvation, the sharp sword of the spirit, feet shod with the gospel of peace, and stand ready to defeat the devil and his army.

People may size you up, and think that you are too small to defeat the giants in your life, but stand! Let them talk! Just as the Israelites didn't think that David could defeat the enemy, he stated that God had delivered him from the paw of the lion and the bear, surely he can deliver me out of the hand of the Philistine! Do you have that confidence in God? Can you stand and defeat the giants in your life? Your giant may be issues in your marriage, finances, relationships, emotional struggles, debt, fear of something, depression, it can be anything. Be encouraged and trust in the Lord with all of your heart. It doesn't matter how big and bad the giant is, you can defeat him and the victory will be in your hand! Some giants/issues are not spiritual, and the only way to defeat the enemy and his tactics, you have to be spiritually minded and fight with the power of God. Ephesians 6:12 "we wrestle not against flesh and blood, but against principalities, against powers, against rulers of the darkness of this world. This fight is not carnal, it's spiritual and the bigger your giant is, the harder it will fall and the victory will be in your hand!

A Cluttered Mind

There is a television show called "Hoarders" that mainly focus on people that live in a house or apartment filled to capacity with clutter. They bring in family members and friends to come in and eventually help the person clean up their mess so they can live a normal life. In the process, they have to throw a lot of things they hold dear to in the trash. This sometimes causes a mental meltdown and sometimes causes them to give up, but by the end of the show, the house is free of clutter and their lives changed forever.

The first thing that comes to mind when we hear the word "clutter" is mess, filth, and piles of items thrown all over the place. Who wants to live in a house filled with clutter? Just looking at a room full of mess can make you feel confused and wonder what caused it to get to that point. There are millions of people walking around every day with a mind that is cluttered with issues and emotions that limit them from being free. A cluttered mind can also limit or bind us from moving forward. Our mind is powerful; it holds thousands of thoughts and dreams and causes us to make decisions and major life changes. Whatever directs our mind, directs our lives. If we allow a person to control our mind, they control our lives. It is very important that we guard our hearts and minds closely so we can be in full control of our lives and available to be used by Christ.

There are issues that clutter our mind and take our focus off of Christ. There is a reason the enemy attacks us in our mind. The enemy uses tactics of the mind in order to destroy us and take us out. The enemy is cunning and crafty, but he has nothing on the power of God. Instead of letting go and allowing God to rid our minds of clutter, we push them to the side and they eventually pile up creating a mess. We often hold on to issues from the past when God has asked us in 1 Peter 5:7 to cast our cares upon him. Issues from the past can sometimes bind us and hold us back. In order to be free from the prison of the mind, we have to release the issues that bind us and limit us. People walk around 365 days a year carrying old issues that weigh them down and produce burdens that pile up like heavy chains. There are some people in our lives we have to let go of in order to be free. It may not feel good, but it is necessary. Issues and feelings of hatred, hurt and resentment due to tragedies from long ago, heartbreak from bad relationships and loss of loved ones, struggles with identity, financial stress, confusion, emotional despair, malice, anger and bitterness, low self - esteem, worry, church hurt, physical and verbal abuse, these things cause the mind to be sick, and limit us from living. The enemy wants us to remain bound, but the power of God can break every chain that has bound us for so long.

Romans 12:2 also remind us to be transformed by the renewing of our minds. This is the key to freedom. We have to renew our minds in order to be what Christ has called us to be. In order to renew our minds, we have to release the issues that bind us. There is an old hymnal that says "Oh what needless pains we bear...all because we do not carry everything to God in prayer..." We have to release those issues to him and allow him to transform our minds and remove the clutter. The unnecessary pains that we bear and the burdens we carry are sometimes because we have not released them unto God. He wants us to cast all of our cares on him. He wants us to be free!

There has to be a major change in order to proclaim freedom in Christ and reap the blessing that he has stored up for us. It's time for a spring cleaning of the mind. Yes, it's time to shift some things around, let go of some people, release issues of the past, and grasp a hold of the freedom that God has provided. In Isaiah 26:3, God promises to keep us in perfect peace, if our mind is stayed on him. Removing clutter from the mind produces freedom in Christ.

THINK ON THESE THINGS

2 Corinthians 5:17 "Therefore if any man be in Christ, he is a new creature; old things are passed away; behold all things are become new.

THINK ON THESE THINGS

Undercover Assignment

"Submit yourselves therefore to God. Resist the devil, and he will flee from you." James 4:7

Being a mother of four wonderful kids, there are lots of movies that we watch on our Family Nights. One of their favorite movies is "Big Momma's House", where Martin Lawrence, a FBI agent, works undercover trying to get information on his suspect and does anything to obtain the information he needs to get the job done. In the end, he apprehends the "bad guy" and justice is served. During the movie, there were times where his identity is mistakenly revealed, but in the end, he accomplishes what he set out to do. Our enemy, the devil, works undercover aiming to assassinate our hopes and dreams and take us out of the will of God. His works undercover using cunning tricks and schemes to destroy the people of God and distract them in any way possible from our main purpose: being fit for heaven.

We know from reading the word of God that the enemy is not on our side. He tries to distract us with worldly desires, and other things that block us from our focus on God. In 1 Peter 5:8, we are reminded to be watchful, because the devil is seeking whom he may devour. His aim is to tear us down and destroy us entirely, but we have the power over him through Jesus Christ. The important thing is to keep believing it. Life and death lies in the power of our tongue. If we speak victory, we shall have it. We have to remain confident that no weapon he forms against us shall prosper (Isaiah 54:17).Romans 8:37 plainly declares that "we are more than conquerors through him that loved us." No matter what plot the enemy has set for us, through faith, we are able to overcome and proclaim the victory in every situation. The enemy sometimes uses the ones we love to betray us. In John 13:21, Jesus plainly pointed that one of his disciples would betray him. Those that we always thought would never do us wrong are sometimes the one that hurt us the most. Many times, we go through major issues and in our weakest hour, the enemy comes in and tries to destroy us. He comes disguised in sheep's clothing pretending that he is on our side, but is an undercover raging wolf trying to complete his assignment.

Yes, there are times when the trials are too much to bear, and it seems there is no way out of the situation at hand. There are times when we feel like our back is against the wall and the enemy has us by the neck, but there is hope. God is able to provide a way of escape and bring total deliverance. There is no need to be fearful, because in all things we must remember that Christ does not desire us to live in fear of what the enemy can do to us. 2 Timothy 1:7: "For God hath not given us the spirit of fear; but of power, and of love, and of a sound mind." Christ equips us with the tools we need to make it through this Christian journey. It is up to us to use what he has given, resist the devil, and in the end make heaven our home.

THINK ON THESE THINGS

Simple Instructions-WAIT!

"I waited patiently for the Lord: and he inclined unto me, and heard my cry." Psalm 40:1

While searching for my first home, I was excited and fell in love with every home that I saw. My parents advised me not to put my hopes in every house I see, but to weigh my options and most importantly, pray to God for guidance. Well, I waited, and I prayed, still no response. I was in my twenties, single, had a full time job, so why can't I find a small home to call my own? I had no luck, so I became impatient and started to complain. One morning as I was preparing for work, God spoke to me! He simply said to me, "wait." I can testify that about a month later, a friend of my father showed me a beautiful mobile home and asked if I was interested. I asked her to give me 2 more weeks to get enough money for a deposit and any other fees she may want. She immediately handed me the keys to the home and told me to start moving in. The favor of God has rested upon me and all because I was obedient to his words and I learned to wait on him.

No matter how long it takes, it will be worth it in the end if you simply wait on him. Hebrews 10:37 "For yet a little while, and he that shall come will come, and will not tarry." God planted those scriptures to remind us that he will do what he promised; we just have to be patient.

THINK ON THESE THINGS

In Genesis 17, God told Abraham that Sara would bear a son. Even though she was of age, God spoke, and it came to pass. Even Abraham, the father of faith, was surprised when God spoke to him about this. Abraham was a hundred years old when his son Isaac was born. With this miracle, God proved to him and everyone that witnessed it, that nothing is too hard for him, and he will bless in his own time, and in his own way. He did for Sarah what he has promised her. Job went through the roughest of times, but in God's time he blessed him with more than he ever had in the beginning. Though he suffered a major loss, and suffered sickness within his body, he remained patient and full of faith that God would come through for him.

Sometimes, moving too fast, or going on our own accord causes us to make the wrong choice and we regret it in the end. We lose out on a lot of things by moving too fast. What do you do while you are waiting? Read your word and pray. His word is filled with encouragement to wait and the results are life changing. Philippians 1:6 "Being confident of this very thing, that he which begun a good work in you will perform it until the day of Jesus Christ:" It may seem like you are at the end of your rope and there is nothing to lose, but wait on the Lord and be of good courage as stated in Psalm 27:14. God will strengthen your heart and increase your faith as he did with Job. Waiting it not always easy, but it is necessary.

You will be able to withstand anything and it will be well worth the wait in the end.

Remember to take God at his word. Yes, he hears you, and he will answer you. He knows our needs before we even ask. He is able to do exceedingly, abundantly above all that we ask or think, but the key to the treasure is simply put into one word…wait.

"Be still and know that I am God" –Psalms 46:10

A Self -Check Up

Many physicians recommend a yearly check-up to make sure everything in our bodies is working as it should. This is a time to discuss any problems we may have and any concerns about our health and wellness. As a believer, we must also perform evaluations or check-ups to make sure our lives are fit for heaven. Spiritual checkups should not be annually, but daily. In our walk with Christ, it is important that we communicate with him and ask him to cleanse us and show us areas that we fall short in.

Last year, I had the opportunity to perform a spiritual check- up on myself and address some major issues that I needed to fix. I want to share with you my personal testimony. God opened my eyes and allowed me to see my flaws and gave me the strength to address them all.

As a Christian, I was content with my life thinking that I was alright in my walk with Christ. I was blessed with a new position at my job where I was surrounded by three dynamic women of God. Each of them possessed a unique quality and as we shared our testimonies we learned from each other and continued to lift each other up in prayer and supplication to God. One of my coworkers shared with us John Bevere's audio drama entitled "Affabel: Window of Eternity". I never heard of it before, and I must say listening to that audio drama caused a major change in my life. As I begin to listen to this drama, I found out there were things that I harbored in my heart that needed to be removed in order to access the kingdom of God.

I was convicted, and for some reason I felt really sad. Through all of this, God was showing me something that I didn't realize I held inside. I had to make a sudden change in my situation and release old feelings of anger and hatred towards people that hurt me in my life. After all, who is worth missing heaven? No one! There were a lot of people in the drama that thought they lived their life according to the Lord's will, but one minor thing caused them to spend eternity in hell. It was shocking to hear that one minor mistake such as not forgiving someone or holding a grudge against someone can cost everything. I definitely did not want to miss heaven because I felt some type of way about people that did me wrong in the past. Forgiving these people and apologizing to them was a hard pill to swallow, but I knew there it had to be done regardless of who was at fault. I wanted to be free from any ill feelings and resentment.

I had a few people in my life that I stopped talking to for years because of twisted drama, and misunderstanding that led to feelings of anger and resentment that I unknowingly held in my heart for quite some time. I did not want to cause any problems, so cutting off all communication with them was my way out. But, after my self-check from the affable series, I found myself trying to decide whether I should go to them and be the bigger person and resolve all ill feelings and apologize or leave well enough alone. When Peter asked Jesus in Matthew 18:21, he asked how many times shall he forgive his brother or sister, Jesus said seventy times seven-it made perfect sense to me.

Whether I did something wrong to initiate the problem or whether I was the victim, I still had to apologize and clear the air because I still had those feelings inside. It took about three days, but I did it!

God is so awesome because with one person I did not even have to say one word. The issue was resolved with only a few words.Glory to God! 2 Chronicles 20:15 was put into action on this assignment.

The word reminds us in that the battle is not ours, it's the Lord's. Anytime we are faced with an issue, as a child of God, he will fight the battle and give us the victory. I challenge you to perform a self-check on your life. Anything that may hinder you from making heaven your home, get rid of it! Anyone that has hurt you in the past, forgive them! It doesn't matter if you are innocent or guilty, you can still make the step and make things right. Whatever it takes, keep your garment without blemish so you can make heaven your home.

THINK ON THESE THINGS

Remember Me

"Cease not to give thanks for you, making mention of you in my prayers;" Ephesians 1:16

Early one morning I woke up crying and my chest felt so heavy. I didn't know what was going on at the time, but I could hear God was speaking to me and I felt strongly to pray for the abused and neglected children all across the world. This seemed strange to me, but I was obedient and went into my living room and began crying out unto God for the children that were victims of rape, kidnapping, neglect and abuse and their families. Once I started praying, I felt a release and I understood that God chose me to intercede on their behalf on that day. I shared this experience with some of my coworkers and it provided strength and encouragement to intercede on behalf of someone else.

In Daniel 9, Daniel fasted, prayed, and wore sackcloth and ashes as he went to God with prayer and supplication. As he prayed unto God he confessed his faults. Not only did he pray for himself, he prayed for all of Jerusalem that God turn away his wrath and that he would provide mercy and forgiveness. In 2 Chronicles 7:1-3, Solomon was sincere in his praying. "When Solomon finished praying, fire came down from heaven, and consumed the burnt offerings and the sacrifices; and the glory of the Lord filled the house.

THINK ON THESE THINGS

We have all heard the phrase "Prayer changed things". Well, it does! Prayer for ourselves as well as others is a way to exercise our faith, compassion, and love for everyone around us. Yes, there are times when we are simply praying for ourselves that God would meet our needs, but it is always good to include others in your prayers. Even when it seems impossible, continue to pray. God is able to do anything but fail. Even things that seem impossible, he can do. In Genesis 25:21, Isaac made a simple prayer to God on behalf of his wife, and the Lord answered his prayer and Rebekah became pregnant. He simply prayed on behalf of someone else, and the Lord honored his request and came through for him.

When I pray in the mornings, I ask God to protect all the troops and their families, as well as those that I do not know that may be lost, confused, afraid, sick, neglected, abused, emotionally torn, and those that are struggling financially. A simple word of prayer can move mountains. Psalms 141:2 says: "let my prayers be set forth before thee as incense: and the lifting of my hands as the evening sacrifice". In the bible days, they used animals as a sacrifice unto God. Times have changed, but the power of prayer has not. We can let our prayers and supplication be a sacrifice unto him as we make our requests known unto God. So, let us pray fervently for one another, make our requests known unto him. Let us continue to pray for one another.

In Need of a Remedy

There are many medications on the market that provide relief for ailments and issues within the body. Most have side effects, and many people have to take additional medication to help with issues caused by side effects. The bible is filled with remedies for any issue that we have physically or spiritually. Anything that we have struggles with, the bible has remedies and with our faith in Christ, we have confidence that it shall come to pass. In James 5:13-15, the word of God shows us the remedies for some of the issues we commonly deal with. "Is there anyone among you afflicted? Let him pray. Is any merry? Let him sing psalms. Is any sick among you? Let him call for the elders of the church; and let them pray over him, anointing him with oil in the name of the Lord. And the prayer of faith shall save the sick, and the Lord shall raise him up; and if he has committed sins, they shall be forgiven him." Trusting in the Lord and believing the words that he has given us is a recipe for success and total deliverance from life's struggles.

Many times we have trouble on every side, seem and it's hard to believe that things will get better, but this is the point where our faith has to be put to work. Christ provides perfect examples in the scriptures to prove to us that he is a man of his word-Elijah prayed that it would rain, and the heavens gave rain causing the earth to produce crops for him-the woman with the issue of blood activated her faith, pressed through the crowd to touch the hem of Jesus' garment and was immediately healed. In his word, he provided remedies for many issues that people were dealing with. In 2 Kings 20, Hezekiah was sick and near death. He was desperate for a change, so he cried out unto the Lord, and he received complete healing and God added 15 years to his life. When Christ provides healing, it is not just a temporary thing like putting a bandage over a scrape or bruise. He provides complete healing and deliverance of any issue.

If you need a remedy for life's struggles, call on the Lord, press your way, and allow him to provide relief. When you go to a doctor for an issue, they write a prescription for something to relieve your ailment. You take it to the pharmacy, and they give you what you need. Prayer is the key, once you reach out to God, he writes your prescription. When you activate your faith and believe that he is able to supply a remedy for your issue, the prescription is filled. The minute you believe, the work is done. When the multitude of witnesses in the bible days came to Jesus for healing, they were healed the minute they believed.

THINK ON THESE THINGS

In Matthew 9:22, Jesus turned to the woman with the issue of blood and told her "your faith has made you whole". Immediately, she was made whole because she was desperate for a change, she saw Jesus, pressed her way, and received what she waited so long to have-relief. The minute she believed, the work was done. Jesus can heal any physical or emotional sickness and disease. With the power that God has given us, we can speak healing and deliverance in our lives and the lives of others with prayer and supplication unto God.

Prayer and Faith Work Hand in Hand

"And whatsoever we ask, we receive of him, because we keep his commandments, and do those things that are pleasing in his sight." -1 John 3:22

Prayer is the one of God's gifts that we often take for granted. Sometimes we sleep or rush through our prayers, not thinking about the words we are saying. Most of the time with our super busy schedules, there isn't much time to pray at all. Prayer is the one thing that we need to make time for as often as possible to make it in these rough times. The end is near, and each time we get a chance, we need to pray. . Sometimes we get consumed with the cares of this world, and prayer can be to some a release and in turn God will provide comfort and meet our requests as we bring them to him. God hears the prayers of the righteous and he assures us throughout the scriptures that he is able to do anything. There is power in prayer. 2 Chronicles 7:1:"When Solomon finished praying, fire came down from heaven, and consumed the burnt offerings and the sacrifices; and the glory of the Lord filled the house."

In prayer, we often tell God what we want, how we want it, when we want it, and forget that he is the head of our lives, and he allows us to have things according to his will. Many times we may want something, but God does not see for us to have it yet. So we have to wait. Waiting is not a hard thing, but it is necessary. With prayer and supplication, we have to include our faith to believe that our request can come to pass. If we pray for a house or car, and we are denied once or twice, does that mean God is not going to give us what we ask for or do we simply wait on him? If we you prayed and asked God for a million dollars, knowing that you have major issues handling finances, never pay tithes, can't keep track of small amounts of money, would you honestly be ready to handle that much money at one time? When God delays our requests, it does not necessarily mean it's a denial. We have to trust him and keep the faith that he will give us what we want in his own time. Reaching out to God is not hard, but he wants us to come to him with the matters of our hearts so he can mend the broken pieces.

Often times we pray for things that are already ours. What we need to do is simply recognize whatever it is need, confess it and believe it. God promises us in John 15:7 that if we abide in him, we can ask what we will and it shall be done. This doesn't mean we can think of anything and we would automatically get it. We often forget that God answers prayers in three ways-no, yes, and wait. The third answer will try our patience, but in the end it works for our good. He plainly shows us what he can do in 2 Chronicles 7:14 "If my people, which are called by my name, shall humble themselves, and pray, and seek my face, and turn from their wicked ways; then will I hear from heaven, and will forgive their sins, and will heal their land." God is able to honor our requests if we are obedient, seek him earnestly and submit ourselves to him. Take him at his word!

"Be careful for nothing; but in everything by prayer and supplication with thanksgiving let your requests be made known unto God" -Philippians 4:6

Rooted and Grounded

Colossians 2:6: "As ye have therefore received Christ Jesus the Lord, so walk ye in him"

In Colossians 2, the apostle Paul wrote to the saints concerning different things regarding their walk with Christ. In Chapter 2, he offered encouragement and reminded them to remember their teachings and apply it to their lives. One of the things he focused on was being rooted and grounded in Christ.

When someone plants a seed in the ground, it develops roots over a period of time. As the plant grows, the roots grow stronger and sometimes go deeper in the ground becoming stable and unmovable. With the proper care, it grows into a beautiful plant blooming with life and ready to produce what it was destined to. As believers, we should be encouraged produce the characteristics of Christ and let our light shine to show the world that Christ is alive and well. Having him as Lord and Savior is the best decision to they will ever make in their lives. Once we have received him as our Lord and Savior, we walk in his ways and we take on his characteristics. His spirit surrounds us daily and bowels of mercy and grace are renewed which provides us with what we need to grow as followers of Christ. We are designed to produce the characteristics of Christ and to share the message of

Christ with the world. Colossians 2:10 reminds us that we are complete in him. We don't have to worry about being malnourished because God provides nourishment and stability so we are able to possess the right fruit and become the child of God that he desires us to be. His spirit will surround us, his goodness and mercy along with his word and truth will fill us with all that we need to grow.

The enemy desires to sift us as wheat, but if we remain rooted and grounded in him, we are able to resist the enemy and his tactics. There may be situations where we may feel alone, confused, hurt, there may be trouble on every side, but don't fret my friend. This too shall pass! Have confidence in knowing that as long as you have Christ on your side and you are rooted and grounded in his word, you have the victory! This is why James 1:2 tells us to count it all joy when we fall into temptations. We are complete in Christ, so there is no need to worry-God has it under control. We must possess the confidence to know that these trials are only temporary and because we are rooted and grounded, we can withstand anything. The victory has already been won all we have to do is allow Christ to dwell in our hearts.

My friend, if you do not know Christ, now is the time to seek him. There is no better time than now to submit to him and allow him to lead you in the path of righteousness. So many things may try to tangle your feet, but hold fast and keep your focus on Christ. These are the last and evil days, and with all the violence and ungodly things appearing every day, it is imperative that all believers are rooted and grounded in Christ. Being secure in Christ is beneficial. When temptation comes and fiery trials seem to be pulling you from side to side, you will not be easily moved. 2 Timothy 4:8 "Ant the Lord shall deliver me from every evil work and will preserve me unto his heavenly kingdom…"

No matter what happens, remember that you are somebody in Christ! Stand firm on the Word of Christ because he is the solid foundation. Continue in the faith grounded and settled, so nothing that comes your way will distract you or move you from the gospel.

THINK ON THESE THINGS

Desperate for Change

Jesus walked the land ministering to multitudes sharing the word of God and providing healing, deliverance, and working mind blowing miracles for those in need. The evidence of his power was made known everywhere. Lives were saved, bodies were healed, dead souls were revived, and because of that many followers believed because of what they witnessed.

Though Jesus is not walking the earth today, he is still able to perform miracles in our lives if we would only have faith and believe. Christ desires us to have faith in him and his ability to perform the same miracles as he did before. He has shown us in his word so many times that he can heal and deliver with just one touch. The people that came to Jesus for relief all had one thing in common. They were desperate for a change in their current situation. Some had been in the same state for years and were looking to Jesus for relief. In Mark 9:17, Jesus was speaking to a multitude of people and someone came to him with a simple request-to help his son who has suffered since childhood with possession by a spirit that hindered him from talking. The child's father even asked the disciples to help cast the demon out, but they could not do it. Now, most people, in that day would think that if the disciples that walked with Jesus could not heal this child, then surely it could not be done. Jesus commanded the demon to leave the child, and immediately the demon was cast out and he began to speak again. The woman with the issue of blood in Luke 8:43 was desparate for healing of her body. She pressed her way when she heard that Jesus was passing by and one touch of his garment gave her complete healing.

I want to speak a word of encouragement to those that may be desperate for change in their lives. There may be things that you have been struggling with for years, you want relief but don't know how to get it. You may be in a toxic relationship and just as the woman with the issue of blood, you may be desperate for Christ to break the chains that has held you bound. Many of you or your loved ones are dealing with addictions, unhealthy habits, and even emotional strongholds that have held you captive. You may feel that you are in a immobile state and are in desperate need for a change.

Change can happen-just one touch can change your entire life. Just as he healed the lame man, the blind man, the woman with the issue of blood, he can do it for you. God is able to loosen the grip that the enemy has over your life and in exchange, he can provide restoration and fill you with his spirit-only if you believe. If you make the first step, he will come in and fulfill your heart's desires. Acts 2:38 is where it all begins.

Once you repent, it opens up the door to a life full of freedom in Christ. The word of God is a roadmap to heaven and he provides keys to defeating the enemy and his tactics. Christ promises to supply our needs if you take the first step and receive him. Matthew 6:33 "but seek ye first the kingdom of God and his righteousness, and all these things shall be added unto you."

"For we brought nothing into this world, and it is certain we can carry nothing out"

Leaving it all Behind

Have you ever seen a U-haul truck behind a hearse? Ever seen a truck or car carrying a deceased loved one's belongings to the cemetery? This sounds a little off the wall, right? No one would ever do that right? There would be no use for earthly belongings when a person has passed away. They are forced to leave it all behind no matter how famous they were or how rich they were. The word of God in I Timothy 6:7 tells us that we brought nothing into this world, and we will carry nothing out. Simply put, the things of this world would be no use in their new home.

The material things that we possess are only temporary. There is no doubt that we need material things in order to make it in this society. The cost of living is high in many areas and in order to provide for our families, we have to have money to pay the bills. Yes, times have changed, but God remains the same. He is still able to supply our needs according to his riches in glory! We all want to have nice things and remain financially stable so we can take care of ourselves and our families. In 1 Timothy 6, the Lord reminds us not to be too attached to it. He advises those of us who many be rich not to be high-minded, not trust in uncertain riches, but rather to trust in God, who gives us things we can enjoy. He doesn't want us to live a boring life, but he gives us things to enjoy. His word promises that he has a cattle on a thousand hill-anything we need, he can provide. Why? Because he is God! There is none like him! It's good to have money and other material things, but don't become too dependent on it.

The main focus is determining where our souls will rest once we depart from this life. Job 14:10 "But man dieth, and waseth away; yea, man giveth up the ghost, and where is he?" God reminds us in his word not to fear what man can do to us because we are only dust. We often spend our time dwelling on the things of this world and obtaining material wealth, when our time should be spent getting our "house in order" so we can have eternal life. "For what is a man profited, if he shall gain the whole world, and lose his own soul? Or what shall a man give in exchange for his soul?" Ever heard the phrase "sell your should to the devil"? If a person offered to give ten million dollars in exchange for your soul, would it be worth it? One could have the pleasures of this world, and never want for anything, but where will their should rest? Job 14:10 asks a very important question.

When a man gives up the ghost, he loses all material things and leaves this earth. From that point, what happens? The answer to that may vary because it depends on the person and their view on life after death. Many believe that there is no heaven or hell. Many believe that we come back in another form ,such as an animal, but the reality is there is a heaven and there is surely a hell. The life that we live will speak for us, and our eternal resting place is based on the work we have done to get our fair reward. At the end of this life, the material things will no longer matter. We will leave all behind our loved ones and our possessions. The only thing that we will carry is our souls. It is imperative that we live a life that is pleasing in the sight of God so we can be assured that heaven will be our home. It's time to reevaluate our lives to ensure we are in good standing with Christ so we can hear those two blessed words: "well done ".

THINK ON THESE THINGS

Spiritual CPR

In emergency situations, mouth-to-mouth resuscitation is required to allow an individual to breathe freely and regain consciousness in an emergency situation. The use of CPR has save thousands of people all across the world. Cardiopulmonary Resuscitation training sessions are available almost anywhere. The certified instructors carefully explain and demonstrate the correct way to perform it in an attempt to help the victim. If applied correctly, the victim can regain consciousness and oxygen will to flow fully to the brain until procedures can be performed to restore the person's heartbeat and breathing. In most cases, the victim is able to regain conciousness. More than 5 minutes without oxygen will cause major brain damage, so this procedure can increase the chances of a full recovery. CPR can save lives.

I remember attending revivals throughout the years, and there was a song that I recall singing at almost every revival. "Revive us Again". This song spoke clearly and reminded us that sometimes we need to be revived. During my 5am prayer session one morning, the word "resuscitate" kept ringing in my ear. As I continued to pray, the Lord showed me a hospital room, and a doctor trying to resuscitate a patient using medical equipment. CPR is sometimes referred to as the "kiss of life".There are times in our lives when we need God to preform a spiritual CPR to help us. He will breathe the breath of life into our situations and break away the things that are not like him, cleansing us from the inside out, causing us to breathe freely and to serve him with no hindrance.

The body of Christ needs to be resuscitated-there are so many people in the body of Christ that are idle, and are not operating in their calling. Their spiritual pulse is low and they need emergency care. This is why it is important for us to pray for one another. Some are suffering from a spiritual cardiac arrest and are silently crying out for help. It may be because of distractions, fear to move forward, the enemy could be choking them in an attempt to make them turn away from God, it could be anything.

I know we can't do it on our own, we need God to perform a spiritual CPR to help us. In the process of God reviving us, he may have to break us away from people or things that may have been blocking us from moving forward in him. Yes, It may not be what we want, but it is necessary in order to be free from unecessary blockage. Sometimes we have to break away from people that mean us no good, even if it is family or close friends. There are people in our lives that have a expiration date, but have yet to "exit the stage". Psalms 138:7 "Though I walk in the midst of trouble, thou wilt revive me." Some relationships and friendships can become toxic and ultimately distracts us from focusing on what is important. God is willing and able to do what it takes to revive us if we allow him to work on us. He will breathe the breath of life into our dead situations and break away the things that are not like him, cleansing us from the inside out, causing us to breathe freely and to serve him with no hindrance.

Do Yourself a Favor and Forgive!

There has to be a major change in order to proclaim FREEDOM in Christ. In order to be free, there has to be a release of things that hold us down. Learning how to forgive is the key. Christ wants us to forgive others as he forgives us. The same way he forgives us for the sins we have committed time and time again we should be just as willing to forgive our brother or sister in the Lord no matter what they did. Nowhere in the bible does it say "well, it depends on what they did to you" he simply says forgive. If you are a Christian, you have been forgiven. We came to God as a filthy rag, and when we repented he washed away all sins and cast them into the sea of forgetfulness- he gave us a clean slate. He treated us as if we never sinned. So why is it so hard for us to forgive one another?

Peter asked Jesus in Matthew 18:21 how many times do I have to forgive my brother?-Jesus said 70 times 7…..Yes, that same person that has slandered your name time and time again, you have to forgive them and pray for them continually. Not only should we forgive others, we have to learn to forgive ourselves also. Yes, there are some things that we have done in our lives that we are not proud of, but there has to be a change in order to become free from the shackles that bind us. Sometimes we are our worst enemy. We bind ourselves at times by the mistakes we made. We ask God for forgiveness for our sins, yet we don't forgive ourselves. We cannot move forward completely until we walk in forgiveness .it is natural to remember the things that happened, or the person that committed such an act, and it seems hard to let go of what happened, but don't let it hold you captive. Forgiveness brings freedom.

The word tells us that Jesus walked with people that secretly despised him. Even at Calvary's cross, he asked God to forgive those people, for they know not what they do. Stephen asked God to forgive the people as they stoned him to death, In Genesis 50, after Joseph's father died, his brothers asked him for forgiveness for the way they treated him –We must do the same as men and women of God. No matter what a person has done or said, we have to forgive them, let it go, and mean it from our hearts not just saying it from our lips. Yes they hurt you, yes they lied on you, or cheated on you, you gave them your heart and they trampled all on it, they scandalized your name, they abused you, they hurt you so bad you are still left in a state of shock-I know u are angry, and it will be hard, but let it go…

Refusing to forgive is toxic. It creates a seed that grows into bitterness, anger, hatred, grudges, thoughts or revenge, or worse! The enemy will have a field day with a person that refuses to forgive. These are not characteristics that Christians should possess. If we plan to make heaven our home, we must remain free of sin, and flee from ungodly thoughts and walk in forgiveness every day. One can say that they have forgiven, but it is the actions that tell the story. Just as love is not known until it's shown, forgiveness is not known until it's shown. If a person that you had issues with years ago walks into a room or comes around you, and it caused your whole attitude or mood to change, then it is apparent that you have not forgiven them. There is still a seed dwelling on the inside that could be toxic. This one thing can cause you to miss out on heaven. Is it worth it? Would all of your living being in vain because you refuse to forgive? Forgiveness is not a feeling; it's a decision. It honestly feels so good to walk in forgiveness!

On a personal note, as I was in the process of writing "Think on these things", I went through one of the worst storms in my life in my marriage. The enemy was on assignment to destroy it along my family, and I had to revert back to the words of encouragement written concerning forgiveness and what to do when the way is not clear. I never thought that I would experience such a deep hurt, but if it wasn't for the Lord, I would not have made it through. I walked in forgiveness, and even though it felt strange, I put aside the feelings of depression, and praised him through the pain. I was in a dark tunnel emotionally, with no light in sight. . It was then that I realized that the blame is not always on the "person", but what is in the person.

The enemy uses anyone to complete his assignment. He uses the ones we love to sometimes hurt us. I had to keep my focus off of the people, but pray that he gives me strength to go through this storm. I still felt "some type of way" concerning the situation I was facing, so I was lead to read James 5:9 "Grudge not one against another, brethren, lest ye be condemned: behold the judge standeth before the door." Reading the word of God provided comfort and initiated the healing process for my storm. The same words that were spoke by God to me to write, I had to apply it to my situation along with consistent prayer and supplication unto God. No, it did not seem fair, but God reminded me that he is the judge, that vengeance belongs to him, and that I needed to stand still and allow him to handle the situation.

I tell you from experience, when your life has been turned upside down by the hands of a person who intentionally hurt you, you still have to let go and forgive. It may not be immediate change, but with prayer and complete faith in Christ, he will guide you and allow forgiveness to be natural-forgiveness brings freedom. In all, we still have to love those that hurt us, even if it is from a distance. If they are in need, the word advises us to have compassion. Yes, in spite of what they did! Romans 12:20: "Therefore if thine enemy hunger, feed him; if he thirst, give him drink; for in so doing thou shalt heap coals of fire on his head".

In this verse, God is reminding us to love without limits! He doesn't want us to be passive or forget what was done, but surprise those who hurt us by loving them! It will shock them, and it may cause a change in their life.

THINK ON THESE THINGS

But Wait...There's More!

There are times when the fog is so heavy, you can't see your way through, but God has spoken and he has heard your prayers, he has seen your tears, he has seen the condition of your wounded heart, and he offers the assurance that THIS STORM WILL NOT CONSUME YOU, this is NOT THE END for you. God is speaking…"Wait, there's more!

Joel 2:21" Fear not O Lord, be glad and rejoice for the Lord will do great things." Many times our trials and tribulations are set to teach us valuable lessons. Tests are set to transition into testimonies. Some things are easier said than done; in the midst of the storm it may be hard to believe that this experience will help someone in the future or even be used as a stepping stone for you to be elevated. Eventually, there will be a story to tell and as always, God will get the glory out of every situation we encounter. Just as the Lord allowed Job to go through extreme trials, in the end, God blessed him with more than he had in the beginning. Job 42:10 "And the Lord turned the captivity of Job, when he prayed for his friends: also the Lord gave Job twice as much as he had before". In the words of my favorite gospel artist Tye Tribbett "If he did it before, he can do it again". Why not trust God? He is more than able to turn a bad situation into a joyous celebration.

THINK ON THESE THINGS

God promises in his word to restore the years that the locust hath eaten-everything that was taken away during your dry season, he is able to restore. Everything that was consumed by the enemy in the storm can be restored. This is a "right now" word for someone and I pray that it reaches YOU! I have been there, I know the deep hurt and emotional scars that can develop after the loss of a loved one, a bad relationship, a tragic event, and living through it is like standing in the middle of a dark tunnel with no light in sight. But wait, God has more! I want to encourage each of you that your best days are ahead of you. It's time to brace yourself, because God is about to blow your mind! This message is intended to lift you up, to provide encouragement through the toughest of time. A lot of times the fog can be described as a "midst", and it is hard to see anything. Joel 3:7 "and ye shall know that I am in the midst...my people shall never be ashamed."

Even in the nastiest of storms, hold your head up high-there is no need to be ashamed of anything. Yes, we all go through hard times, but God is saying wait my child, there is more! I have more for you if you just hang on a little while longer. 2 Corinthians 4:17: "For our light affliction, which is but for a moment, worketh for us far more exceeding and eternal weight of glory" Verse 18 encourages us to focus on the things which are not seen. This is where you have to apply your faith and increase your confidence that HE WILL come through and you will come out of this as pure gold. You may not be able to see it, but it's because the fog seems to be the thickest at the end of the tunnel. Hold on, you are one step closer to VICTORY, one prayer away from DELIVERANCE, one dance away from HEALING, one more praise away from FREEDOM and HAPINESS through Christ.

Now is the time to stand boldly and declare the word of God "Persecuted, but not forsaken"-he promises in his word to never leave us or forsake us...you may be cast down, but not destroyed. Lamentations 2:16 "all thine enemies have opened their mouths against me..." It may seem as if you are about to be devoured by the enemy, but wait, there's more! God is not through yet. Just as he kept the lion's mouth closed as he was cast in the lion's den, he is able to make your enemies behave and they will in turn become your footstool. 1 Peter 4:13 "But rejoice, inasmuch ye are partakers of Christ's sufferings when his glory shall be revealed, ye may be glad also with exceeding joy."

The word of God provides comfort and encouragement no matter what the situation may be. Count it all joy....it will be well worth it in the end. He has proven his power many times throughout the scriptures, and he still reigns today and is able to do more than we could ever imagine. The key is to "give it to him". He has been known to heal the sick, raise the dead, feed the hungry, cast out spirits, part the Red Sea, and so much more. He is able to do it! All of your worries, all of your struggles, all of those sleepless nights, pillow wet with tears, it can all be dissolved if you would only step aside and allow him to take your burdens and all of your cares. One of my favorite hymnals has a key verse in it that I never understood completely until I knew Christ for myself. "Oh what needless pains we bear…all because we do not carry everything to God in prayer." We carry unnecessary weights and drag heavy baggage from the past when Christ clearly advises us to cast our cares upon him.

This is definitely not the end for you, he is able to provide peace in the midst of your storm. The only thing that is required of us is to mentally let go of the situation and allow him to come in and heal the hurt, heal the pain, wash away your tears, and provide strength. He is able to give us strength in our weakness. Even when it seems like the weight of the world is on our shoulders, we can find comfort in Lamentations 3:22: "It is of the Lord's mercies that we are not consumed, because his compassions fail not".

Before you even think about throwing in the towel, calling it quits, turning your back on the situation and allow it to consume you, think about all the love that God has for you. Seek refuge in Christ. He is waiting on you to give it to him. Lamentations 3: 25 "The Lord is good to them that wait for him, to the soul that seek him". You may be in a bad place now, and the odds seem to be against you, your back may even be against the wall right now, but just know that he has not forgotten you, he is there, and he sees what's going on. "Proverbs 3:5-6: "Trust in the Lord with all your heart, and lean not unto your own understandings... In all thy ways acknowledge him, and he shall direct thy paths." Think about the testimony that will come out of this test- you may even be able to help someone get through the same trial in the future. My prayer is that you hold on, keep the faith, take God at his word, and smile because your joy will come in the morning!!! He knows all about it, he has seen your tears, and he is ready, willing, and able to turn your struggle into victory. Be encouraged! Brace yourself, God is about to blow your mind!

Stay on the Line

"Therefore, brethren, stand fast, and hold the traditions , which ye have been taught, whether by word, or our epistle" II Thessalonians 2:15

Have you ever gone to someone for advice, and they always know the right words to say? The advice they give seems right on time, and it's just what the doctor ordered. It's good to have someone who knows just what to say to help us in our everyday lives.. Living in the last days, it is imperative that we are careful as to what we hear and who we follow. There are many deceivers around, and their aim is to lead us away from Christ so we won't make it to heaven. There are times where the word we hear is not necessarily the word from the Lord.

"For the time will come with they will not endure sound doctrine; but after their own lusts shall they heap to themselves teachers, having itching ears" II Timothy 4:3. We are living in the last days, and there are now deceivers led by divers spirits lurking in an attempt to destroy ministries and distract believers everywhere. These spirits try to shift the voice of God and deceive them with words that seem right because they sound nice when they are actually wrong,. Some preachers are still preaching the true word of God, but beware for those that "tickle your ears with things that don't line up with the word of God. In Colossians 2: 8, he warns us to "Beware lest any man spoil you through philosophy and vain deceit, after the tradition of men, after the rudiments of the world, and not after Christ." These words are not meant to scare us, but simply to keep us on alert so we can discern what is real versus what is not.

Be mindful that God has not given us the spirit of fear... (II Timothy 1:7) He wants us to be bold and spread his message of love everywhere we go. The news reports lately have shown several people being killed in other counties because they refused to denounce Christ and convert to their religion. There will be times when we will be punished, and sometimes persecuted for his name's sake. It is imperative that we stay on the line, and continue to trust and believe in the word of the Lord no matter what. Matthew 24:13 confirms to us that "he that shall endure unto the end, the same shall be saved". There are many benefits in staying on the line and keeping the faith. God's word was the same yesterday, will stand the same today, and forever more. Even when it seems that we are leaning to the left or the right, his words gives us the confidence that he will be our helper and our shield if we would trust in him (Psalm 115:11).

Have Some Fruit

Galatians 5:22-23: "But the fruit of the spirit is love, joy, peace, longsuffering, gentleness, goodness, faith, meekness, temperance: against such there is no law"

In order create a fruit salad, one must cut and mix different varieties of of fruit to create a delicious dish. One dish, many ingredients. One of my favorite scriptures in Galatians talks about the fruit of the spirit. For a long time, I would hear the scripture read, but I never understood that it was the "fruit" of the spirit not the "fruits" of the spirit. Many characteristics join together to make up the fruit of the spirit. These are characteristics that we must possess as a believer. It is very important to have these in mind and apply them to our lives each day. By doing this, we can produce good fruit. An apple tree produces apples, a pear tree produced pears, a Christian produces "Christ-like" characteristics. People can tell that you have the Holy Spirit on the inside by the fruit you bear. With Christ in your life, you have no other choice than to bear good fruit. Christ commands us in Matthew 5:44 to love our enemies and he proclaims in 1 John 3:11 "For this is the message that ye heard from the beginning, that we should love one another."

It may seem hard to love someone that hurts you, or has done you wrong, but the love of Christ will condition your heart and mind to forgive, and will provide peace that will surpass all understanding. In order to have the fruit of the spirit, one must have love. People may see you and not understand why you are able to smile and love a person who hurt you in the past, but the love of Christ dwelling in you will cover a multitude of sin, remove any ill feelings, and allow you to walk in forgiveness and in the newness of life. There are times we have to suffer. Situations push us to the limit, but we must endure in the face of difficulty –that is longsuffering. Longsuffering can be seen as putting up with people and circumstances and not fall into sin. Walking by the spirit produces the fruit of the spirit. Bearing good fruit is a sure sign that the Holy Spirit dwells on the inside. Christ wants us to maintain temperance so when trouble arises, we are calm enough to understand that "vengeance is mine saith the Lord".

We have to be gentle like the Good Samaritan and allow our gentleness to manifest in every aspect of our lives. Gentleness ties in with meekness. The gentleness of God leads people to change. You can't have one without the other. "Blessed are the meek; for they shall inherit the earth (Matthew 5:5) "Brethren, if a man be overtaken in a fault, ye which are spiritual, restore such a one in the spirit of meekness; considering thyself, lest thou also be tempted. Being meek produces positive results. Our faith increases with each trial that we endure. The words of Christ in Matthew 17:20 clearly tells us if we have a small grain of faith, we can move mountains (no matter how large the mountains are). Nothing shall be impossible, as long as we recognize the measure of faith that he has given each of us. Think about an apple tree. Once it begins to grow, it starts to produce apples. Once we, as believers, accept Christ as our Lord and Savior, the journey begins. Just as a seed is planted, we nurture ourselves with the proper teaching, studying, and with the proper prayer life, we will grow into a strong believer with a great measure of faith, and implanted with the power of the Holy Ghost.

Just as the sun provides light to plants to help them grow, we have to use the light of Christ and "let our lights shine before men… (Matthew 5:16) We cannot have any fleshly manifestation on the inside such as fornication, adultery, hatred, envy, jealousy, wrath, strife, heresies, or anything not like God. By standing strong as a believer of Jesus Christ and allowing the characteristics of Christ effectively manifest in our lives each day, we produce the Fruit of the Spirit.

Hot or Cold?

In my daily readings, I came across an amazing scripture about a young king who served God, but not with his whole heart. In II Chronicles chapter 25, we learn about the 8th king of Judah. Amaziah was a young king, and he did what was right in the sight of the Lord, but not with a perfect heart. He did what he wanted to do, even if it meant not listening to the direction of the Lord. A lot of times people strattle the fence and serve God when it is convenient for them, sort of like a part time lover. We can all recall a time when we did something for someone and our heart was not in it. I used to be a people pleaser, and I did many things to please people when my heart was not in it. I didn't change my ways until I found Christ as my Lord and Savior. In this amazing scripture, it seemed that King Amaziah had a heart to serve God, but he still had something that kept him from being completely tuned into the will of the Lord. A lot of times, we harbor ill feelings or issues of the past that keep us from being 100% with God. We serve him part-time but want full time benefits and blessings. Amaziah seemed to have some type of anger in his heart towards the people that killed his father, Joash. Once he was settled in as king, he killed the servants and ll those that had killed his father as an act of revenge.

There are people who have done things to purposely hurt our loved ones, but that doesn't give us the right to take matters in our own hands. Life is full of ups and downs, but as a believer we have to remain faithful that God will handle it. The word of God tells us that "vengeance is mine saith the lord". That simply means leave it alone, "I got this!". During Amaziah's reign his pride got the best of him. He acted out of his own thoughts instead of following God's words. He even worshipped the gods of Edom.God became angry in the 15th verse and he sent a prophet to him to speak a word-he still didn't listen. In the end, he turned away from God and he ended up being murdered.

On a hot day, would u rather a nice cold cup of ice water, or a lukewarm cup of water to quench your thirst? Well, it's the same thing when thinking about our relationship with God. Revelation 3:15 "basically talks about being "lukewarm". He does not desire us to be lukewarm or serve him selectively. His word warns us that he will spew us out of his mouth. You either serve God, or you serve the devil. The proof is in the word of God! Matthew 6:24 "No man can serve two masters: for either he will hate the one, and love the other, or else he will hold to the one, and despise the other..." In Amaziah's case, he had good intentions in the beginning, but eventually clinged to the world's way and turned his back on God. His pride led to his downfall. In the end, lost out on being a mighty man of God.

The words of Christ in Matthew 15:8: "this people draweth nigh unto me with their mouth, and honoreth me with their lips; but their heart is far from me." Christ does not intent for us to put on a show for others or to pretend that we are saved and filled with his Holy Spirit. There are many people that are simply "playing church". They live how they want to all week long, then on Sunday they want to give God lip service and praise him with everything but their heart. God is seeking real worshippers.

I challenge each of you to serve the Lord with all of your heart, mind, and soul. No matter what comes or what goesIf you get weak along the way, hold on! You may be moving at a slow pace, but keep going! Live according to his ways and reap the benefits as a child of God. Dare to be real! Pray that he gives you clean hands, and a pure heart (Psalms 24:4)so that you will be able to serve him wholeheartedly and he will be pleased with your service. Do what is right in his sight every day and be what God has called you to be.

Putting All of Your Trust in Him

Have you ever seen kids play a game where they fall back and the person standing behind them catches them? The individual leaning has all trust that they will not fall and their friend will catch them. What if that person did not serve their purpose of holding you up and caused you to fall? How would you feel? Would you be shocked that they left you hanging or possibly did this on purpose? Many times we put our faith and trust in people that do not have out best interest in mind. They say they will be there and will always stand behind us, but when the time arises when we need help, they are nowhere to be found. We assume because they are made to serve a specific purpose in our lives and they have never let us down before , they will always be there . Not all the time. There are some genuine friends who will stick by you, but there are many that you cannot trust. What is trust? Trust is a powerful word and is often taken for granted. Do you know the true meaning of trusting someone? To say that you trust someone means that you have confidence and completely rely on them.

God wants each of us to rely on him and to remain confident that he will take care of us. Proverbs 3:5-6: "trust in the Lord with all your heart, and lean not unto thine own understanding. In all thy ways acknowledge him, and he shall direct thy paths." These words should open up our understanding more concerning God's plans for our lives. He assures us through his word that if we only trust and lean on him, we don't have to worry about what to do, when to do it, or which way to turn because he will direct our paths and lead us in the right way as long as we trust him and acknowledge him in everything that we do. Yes, some tough situations may arise where we may not understand the answer that God has set before us. We may not always like the answer he gives when we pray for help. We have to be reminded that we should not lean on our own understanding because we may be thinking carnal at the moment "For to be carnally minded is death; but to be spiritually minded is life and peace" Romans 8:6 When your mind operates in the flesh, you cannot please God. We have to be spiritually minded in all things.

People let you down, things don't always go as planned, and sometimes you will have to hang your head and cry, but never question why? God will always be there no matter what. He will never let you down or lead you in the wrong path. He promises to never forsake or leave us. It's comfortable to trust God when you are doing well, but can you trust him when you lost everythingh, when your money has run out, when your relationship is destroyed, when you can't see the light at the end of the tunnel? Have you ever heard the saying "Trust him even when you can't trace him"? Yes, sometimes the storms of life are so bad that it seems that God is not there, or that he has forgotten about you, but he is ALWAYS there no matter what. This is why we should rejoice and be confident in him. Yes, you can trust him even when things don't go your way. Psalms 5:11 "But let those that put their trust in thee rejoice, let them ever shout for joy because thou defendeth him" He promises to fight for us and in every situation, give us the victory. His word did not say we would not go through hard times, but he did promise us that our weeping may endure for a night, but in the morning we shall have JOY-this is why he tells us to rejoice in our tribulation. Yes, we all will go through, but at the end of the day he shall increase us more and more (Psalm 115:14). Do you trust him?

"Ye that fear the Lord trust in the Lord: he is our help and our shield" Psalms 115:11

Thank You for Covering Me

I was headed home from work and took an alternate route. 5 o'clock traffic was backed up, and I was waiting at the light when all of a sudden a van came flying fast through the red light and hit a car causing it to flip several times uncontrollably. I was in a state of shock because it was right in front of me and immediately prayed for the persons involved. I knew in my heart that it was God's grace that no one was seriously hurt, and if I had arrived at the light a few seconds earlier, it could have been me. There are many times that God shields us from things that could have consumed us. Lamentations 3:22 " It is of the Lord's mercies that we are not consumed, because his compassions fail not".

If we had the ability to glance at the unseen dangers that God shields us from on a daily basis, it would blow our minds. His mercy and his grace cover us daily even when we are not worthy. We know that the devil has his workers on assignment every day seeking to kill, steal, and destroy us by any means necessary. Anything or anyone in our lives that takes from us that steals our joy, that aims to destroy our purpose is not of God. The enemy often uses the ones closest to us to hurt us, and distract us from our focus. This is why we should always watch and pray. It is imperative that we, as believers, continue to pray and seek God daily that he would bless and protect us from the hands of the enemy. Think about those of us that are   riding on the highway each day. There is only one thin line that separates one car from the next. At any given time, one can cross over to the next lane causing an accident, but God's grace and mercy allows us to make it safely each day. Each of us can think right now of one situation in our lives where we should have gone to jail, or should have been dead, or should have lost everything, but God turned things around and covered us with his grace and with his never ending mercy. Every chance that we get, we should give him praise for being our shield and being so merciful. What could have taken me out, didn't and it is because of his grace that covered me.

We should live our lives as a "thank you" for all of the marvelous things that he does for us. There are times that we don't deserve his mercy, but he wraps us in his amazing grace and his mercy. Even in our mess, he is able to shield us from the things that we cannot see. God loves each of us, and each morning his mercies are renewed-he covers us even when we don't realize it.

THINK ON THESE THINGS

Meekness vs. Weakness

"For the meek shall inherit the earth; and shall delight themselves in the abundance of peace" Psalm 37:11

As I was studying meekness, I came across the word "weak. If meekness is a part of who we are in Christ, then how can weakness be associated it? Meekness is definitely not weakness! Being meek does not mean that everyone can walk all over you. It is definitely not a sign of weakness. I started to think about the times in my life where I felt like a doormat. Many times, I have personally felt like that and for a long time, people took advantage of my kindness and gentleness. They used those characteristics in me to get what they wanted.

At the time I didn't realize it, but the reason I felt that way was mainly the result of my own low self- esteem and lack of self-worth. I became a people pleaser and in a way, my meekness was actually looked to as weakness. For years, I struggled with these feelings and it wasn't until I completely submitted to the will of God that I was delivered from those feelings. Meekness is definitely not Weakness. Let's talk a little bit about meekness.

What does meekness look like? The meekness that Jesus talks about in the word of God is all positive. Matthew 5:5 clearly states "blessed are the meek: for they shall inherit the earth…" To get the best view of meekness, look in the word of God. True meekness is a love that values others more than one's self. In the word of God, Jesus was known to tirelessly help the crowds of people that flocked to him. You can see meekness when a Christian turns the other cheek. Christians become more meek the more the Holy Spirit teaches them to be like Jesus.

An inheritance usually comes after someone has died. The word of God says that "the meek shall inherit the earth..."Think about it. Since Jesus died on the cross for us, not only are all of our sins forgiven, but we also have the promise that everything in the world is working for our good. We find joy as we inherit the earth. It was promised to us in the word find joy as

Promises Fulfilled in His Time

"This day the Lord thy God hath commanded thee to do these statutes and judgements; thou shalt therefore keep and do them with all tine heart, and with all thy soul." Deuteronomy 26:16

The Lord spoke to Moses several times with specific instructions concerning the Children of Israel. In the book of Leviticus, there are many declarations made and promises that he advised Moses that he would do if the people kept his commandments. There were also some "not so good" promises that he made if they did not follow his instructions and walk in his ways. Many times in life we are disappointed by the broken promises that we have made or that others have made to us. One thing is sure, God's promises are never broken. His word will never return void. There is joy in reading the word of God and hearing his promises to us if we keep his word. Leviticus 26:3-4 "if ye walk in my statutes, and keep my commandments, and do them; then I will give you rain in due season and the land shell yield her increase, and the trees of the field shall yield their fruit." This passage of scripture is bursting with wonderful promises and benefits from the Lord concerning us. Further down in verse 6 he promises to give us "peace in the land". If we look at his word in our spiritual eyes, we can see the abundance of blessing that pour out of his word.

THINK ON THESE THINGS

God promises to bless us in his own time. A lot of times we try to rush God, we want things to happen immediately. There is no time limit when it comes to God. He may not come when we want him, but when he shows up; trust that it was his appointed time. We often become impatient and end up losing our focus because things don't happen when we want it to. Let's look at it in a different view. When you bake a cake, there is a timer that you can set that will sound once the cake is done. There is a precise time you expect it to be complete. In a spiritual view, God sets the timer for us, but we are not able to see it. He will release it to us in HIS TIME. His delay cannot be mistaken for his denial. A lot of times, we are not mentally or spiritually ready for what God has for us. When it is time, his favor and blessings will pour down and we shall yield our increase Ezekiel 36:11 reminds us that he will do better unto us than our beginning. Just like the story of Job, our latter will be much greater than our beginning. God is able to do anything but fail. He can give us double for our trouble. This is why he encourages us to rejoice in tribulation.

It's hard to smile or to feel joy as we endure hardships, but there is comfort in knowing that we will reap great things in due season. Yes, there are times when we will go through dry seasons, desolate places in our lives, but his promises will be fulfilled. Ezekiel 37:14 "..And shall put my spirit in you, and ye shall live…" Even in the process of creating this devotional, I was in a dry place. I thought that I was going to lose it, but I had to focus on Psalms 91 and remind myself that if he began a good work in me, he will perform it. If he promised me that he would bring me out, I have to activate my faith and wait on him! It was not easy, and it was extremely uncomfortable, but in due season he showed me that he is able to do ANYTHING! He proved his word to be true, and I am able to testify of his works and encourage others from my experiences.

God's gives us affirmations to live by and the evidence validates his magnificent power. What a mighty God we serve! Deuteronomy 28:12 "The Lord shall open unto thee his good treasure, the heaven to give the rain unto thy land in his season, and to bless all the work of thy hand: and thou shalt lend unto many nations; and thou shalt not borrow."

Nobody is Exempt

"For the wages of sin is death, but the gift of God is eternal life through Jesus Christ our Lord." -Romans 6:23
On the first day of school, teachers and administrators across the country review the classroom rules and explain the punishment for not following the rules. Sometimes, there are harsh punishments that come as a result of disobedience. When I was in school, one of my forms of punishment was to write on the chalkboard 100 times "I will not sleep in class". It was hard, but I had to give up my recess with the rest of my peers and spend the entire time paying for the wrong I did. After all, that is fair, right? The same applies to our walk with Christ.

God created specific rules for us to live by. The Ten Commandments specify the things he does not want us to do. In the word of God, there are also consequences to being disobedient to God's commandments. No one is exempt. God is fair in all things and his word is true. ". Even the angels that reigned with him were punished for any sin they committed. In II Peter 2:4, it clearly shows that no one is exempt from punishment: "For if God spared not the angels that sinned, but cast them down to hell, and delivered them into chains of darkness to be reserved to judgement God has no favorites. He punished many in the bible days for their disobedience. He destroyed Sodom and Gomorrah, he punished Adam and Eve for their disobedience, and the list goes on. No one is exempt from punishment. Jeremiah 21:14 "Bur I will punish you according to the fruit of your doings saight the Lord; and I will kindle a fire in the forest thereof, and it shall devour things round about it. "There are some that may believe that God is too good and merciful to punish anyone or sentence them to hell. He established commandments for us to live by, and those who do not abide by them have to deal with the consequences. Simply put, "the wages of sin is death..." (Romans 6:23). He paved the way for us! Many will not accept him and may end up losing out on heaven.

Many think that because they are doing ungodly things behind the scenes, nothing will happen to them. We may not be able to physically see it, but God sees and knows everything. Nobody is perfect and his word in Titus 3:3 tells us that we ourselves are sometimes foolish, disobedient, deceived, but when God sent his son Jesus Christ to die on the cross of Calvary to cover our sins, it cleaned our slates! We have access to heaven if we accept him. Salvation is free! We are justified by graced and freed from the bondage of sin. He was merciful enough to allow us a second chance to walk in the newness of life. In his word, God promises to bless us with long life and if we accept him as Lord and Savior, follow his commandments, and live according to his commandments, we shall receive the greatest gift ever- eternal life.

THINK ON THESE THINGS

God loves us so much, and he doesn't want to see any of us go to hell. He urges us throughout the scriptures to live right, obey his commandments, and he desires us all to "make it in". He loves us and he considers us as sons and daughters. If he did not chasten us, we would be unruly and out of order. We would surely be hell-bound. Think about it. Parents discipline their children because they want the child to grow up and develop good character. God wants us to possess Christ-like characteristics and he disciplines us in his own way because he loves us.

THINK ON THESE THINGS

What's in Your House?

There are many catchy phrases or symbols that we remember from commercials over the years. One that came to mind was the catchy phrase "What's in your wallet?" I immediately thought about the commercial for the Capital One credit card. The point of the phrase was to encourage consumers apply for one of their credit card. It made me think about the question that was asked of the widow in II Kings 4. She was asked "what's in your house" when she told the man of God that she was a widow and had many debts. She had no way to pay them, so the creditors were coming to take her 2 sons to be bondsmen. The point of him asking this question was to encourage the widow to use the oil she had to get what she desired. Ever heard the saying "Use what you got?" It speaks volumes when it comes to the word of God.

II Kings 4 (KJV): 2 "And Elisha said unto her, What shall I do for thee? Tell me, what hast thou in the house?". We all are familiar with this story. God provided just what she needed and her obedience to the man of God allowed her to have enough to pay her debt and more left over. One of the things that stuck with me was the instruction to "shut the door". The only thing that she had was a pot of oil. Elisha instructed her to borrow some vessels from her neighbors and in II Kings 4 verse 4, he told her to shut the door and pour the oil into all the vessels and set aside those that were full. Even though she had only a pot of oil, the Lord provided enough for her to fill up all the vessels and more left over. He filled her up to capacity-he took what she had in the house, and blessed her.

A lot of times God gives us instructions and in order for us to receive our blessings, we have to shut the door. Nothing personal, but at times, you have to isolate yourself from others in order to get what you need from the Lord. In the widow's case, she had to follow the man of God and shut the door and follow instructions. Think about it. If the widow had nosey neighbors that came in asking questions, they would have placed doubt in her mind and distracted her from receiving what God had in store for her. Though it didn't look like there was enough oil, there was an overflow and it was all because of her obedience and faith. Anything could have happen if she had not shut the door. Think about that nosey neighbor that would have came knocking at the door asking crazy questions. "How can u fill all these vessels up with that small amount of oil?" Sometimes you can't let everyone know what you are doing because it will mess things up and open the door to doubt and fear. If Noah didn't follow God's instructions, would there have been an ark? If the blind man did not follow Jesus' instructions, would he have received his sight?

Matthew 17:20 reminds us that if we have faith as small as a mustard seed, we can move mountains and nothing will be impossible. God is able to do anything for us if we believe. The same way Jesus fed the five thousand with only 2 fish and 5 loaves of bread, he can provide for us. He is a miracle worker and with the activation of our faith in him, and being obedient to his words, his word says he can give us the desires of our heart. What's in your house? Do you carry the faith to take God at his word even though it looks impossible? The widow was in need, and she received what she needed and more from the Lord.

HE WILL DO WHAT HE SAID

Philippians 4: 19: "But my God shall supply all your need according to his riches in glory by Christ Jesus."

Many restaurants that offer delivery give an estimated time to expect the order. If it has not arrived in the expected time, one can call to verify the order or simply go pick it up. In the Word of God, we find that God works in his time, not in ours. Many miracles that Jesus performed were quick, but it was in the appointed time. James 1:6 reminds us to ask in faith. The woman who had an issue of blood had struggled for twelve long years with no relief. In her appointed time, she was able to receive her healing. She got close enough and at the right time, she received what she desired.

In the book of Exodus we see where God had compassion on the people who dwelled in Egypt and he delivered them in his appointed time. Time is such a precious thing, and when God says he will do something, he will follow through with it. Exodus 3:7 "And the Lord said I have surely seen the affliction on my people which are in Egypt, and have heard their cry..." further down in verse 9 he promises to deliver them out of the hands of the Egyptians and place them in a land that flowed with milk and honey. God sensed the affliction of his people and further in the word it shows that he did just what he said. He took them out of a bad situation and placed them into a land flowing in abundance. He provided deliverance in his time. There may be times that we seem to linger in a bad place, but be confident that God is able to do what seems impossible. There may even be times that we spiritually feel that we are left alone, but when we need help we need to be confident and understand that our trust lies in the Lord and not in man. God has proved him He is able to deliver out of a dry place and into a place of safety. He also promises in Joel 2: 26 "and ye shall eat in plenty, and be satisfied..." There is nothing too hard for God and in his appointed time, he is able to provide healing, deliverance, peace, and safety if we call out to him. He is compassionate and understands the struggle.

His word is sure and he reminds us that he will do what he said. No matter what the situation is, he promises to fulfill his word. Look at what he promises in Isaiah 55:11: "so shall my word be that goeth forth out of my mouth: it shall not return to me void, but it shall accomplish that which I pleased and it shall prosper in the thing whereto I sent it."

The Harvest is Plentiful

"The sluggard will not plow by reason of the cold; therefore shall he beg in harvest and have nothing" Proverbs 20:4

As a child, I can recall many Saturday mornings my siblings and I would sleep late or just lay in the bed and watch TV. Mom would come in the room and remind us "half the day is gone, yall aint done nothing! Get your lazy butt up, and do something!" She always reminded of us of the many chores there were waiting on us and we needed to get out of the habit of being lazy. At the time, we didn't like being called lazy, but as adults we can appreciate it and teach our families to be active and not become a lazy person. No one wants a lazy person on their team, right? A team filled with lazy people will always come up last because they don't have a "get up and go" mentality. In a spiritual view, God wants each of us to abstain from being idle or lazy and to be about his business. When a person accepts Christ as their Lord and Savior, they become a member of the body of Christ. This is not a physical body, but in a spiritual view, Christ is the head, and we as believers are members that make up the body of Christ. It can also be viewed as a large garden…and we have to keep our spiritual bodies in good maintanance without spot or wrinkle so we can reap in harvest time.

THINK ON THESE THINGS

The harvest is plentiful, but the laborers are few. God wants us to get to work in his kingdom. Harvest time in a spiritual view is when Christ comes for us, his church, and welcomes us into the kingdom of heaven. We all have to be judged before we can gain access. We have to show our works and present to him a blameless, spotless soul. The word of God is designed to help each of us along the way so that we can make heaven our eternal home. It is important, as a believer, to be active in the works of the Lord. Think of it like an actual garden. If two neighbors plant gardens each year and they are known to have plenty in harvest time. What happens if one neighbor doesn't plant his garden-in harvest time, he has nothing to reap. The word of God doesn't show the word "lazy", but it refers to it as slothful or sluggish. Let's take a look at the word. Proverbs 20:4 "the sluggard will not plow by reason of cold; therefore he shall beg in harvest and have nothing." In Proverbs the "reason of cold" is referring to the time that they plowed. Back in those times, the Palestines plowed in late October-early November and they sowed their seeds, kept maintenance of them until it was time to reap the harvest. The word of God reminds us that if we become lazy and make excuses for not doing anything, when it is time to reap our reward or to show the Lord what we have done, we have nothing to show. Proverbs 21:25: "the desire of the slothful killeth him; for his hands refuse to labor." This slothful man is eaten up/killed because he has no willingness to work.

His desire for his harvest /blessing will only come with work, and without it, he has nothing. How can you gather a harvest if nothing was ever planted? In another view, how can a person earn a paycheck if they never worked? If nothing was sowed, what is there to reap?

Laziness or slothfulness is definitely not godly. God wants us to be about his business. Even in Judges 18:9 it mentions slothful: ..."be not slothful to go and possess the land." In order to possess the land, one has to get u up, and go get it! "He wants us to be excited about serving him, not sluggish and uninterested. Being a believer is a privilege and we may not have the same job/position, but the work that we do is just as important as another. ("Many members, but one body. Remember, the harvest is plentiful, but the laborers are few. Are you a laborer?

THINK ON THESE THINGS

ABOUT THE AUTHOR

Teresa Richardson was born and raised in Bishopville, South Carolina to Bishop Nathaniel and Mary Dixon. The second oldest of five children, she always had a passion for helping others. Teresa is married with four beautiful children and loves to inspire people that she comes into contact with daily. She enjoys singing, teaching Sunday school at her father's church, couponing, and working with kids. Her passion is helping others and that is what she feels God has called her to do. Teresa was inspired to write a parable type devotional back in 2012. Doubt, hesitation and fear set in and it delayed the process. With prayers and encouragement from close friends, family, and church, she finally birthed the inspirational words that God has given her with hopes that it will bring life to someone's situation and draw them closer to Christ.

Pure Thoughts Publishing, LLC

www.ingramcontent.com/pod-product-compliance
Lightning Source LLC
Chambersburg PA
CBHW071535040426
42452CB00008B/1028